Know and Believe

Know and Believe

A Lifetime Journey toward
Rediscovering God's Love for You

By
C. D. Hildebrand

Xulon Press

Xulon Press
2301 Lucien Way #415
Maitland, FL 32751
407.339.4217
www.xulonpress.com

Definitions of Greek words, unless stated otherwise, are derived from Strong's Concordance.

It is not essential to look up the Bible references within parenthesis unless you want to know why a certain statement is correct. Scripture essential to understanding the concepts in this book is written out for your convenience.

The author chose not to use gender-specific pronouns unless specifically indicated, as she finds writing and reading "he/she," "him/her," and "his/hers" to be tedious. Please assume any truth applies to both genders even though he, him, his, or mankind are used.

www.xulonpress.com

Printed in the United States of America.

ISBN-13: 9781545645208

*This book is dedicated
to all believers in Jesus Christ
who treasure God's love
more than life.*

Table of Contents

Know and Believe

**A Lifetime Journey toward
Rediscovering God's Love for You**

This Book is for You If xi
Foreword xiii
Acknowledgements xvii
Prologue xxi
Introduction xxiii
God Loves You xxvii

PART ONE: His Love on Display

Chapter 1 The Journey Home 33
Chapter 2 Creation and the Fall 45
Chapter 3 God's Heart of Love 49
Chapter 4 Understanding Covenants 53
Chapter 5 The Law's Loving Purpose 59
Chapter 6 The Prophets, Gospels, Psalms, and Proverbs . . . 67
Chapter 7 He is Who He Claims to Be 75

PART TWO: No Greater Love

Chapter 8 The Fulness of Time 83
Chapter 9 The Appearance of His Love 88
Chapter 10 If You've Seen Me 92
Chapter 11 No Greater Love 100

Chapter 12 Nothing Can Separate Us 105
Chapter 13 Seeking God's Love. 109
Chapter 14 Blessed 115

PART THREE: Experiences that Seek to Extinguish

Chapter 15 Limited Love 125
Chapter 16 Abusive "Love" 133
Chapter 17 Rejection 137
Chapter 18 When Life Wears Us Down 143
Chapter 19 Unrealistic Societal Expectations 148
Chapter 20 Long-term Struggles 156
Chapter 21 Abuse by Spiritual Authorities 168

PART FOUR: Teachings That Nullify

Chapter 22 False Perceptions and Accusations 181
Chapter 23 Horror Instead of Hope 187
Chapter 24 Conditional Love 198
Chapter 25 Never Complete. 206
Chapter 26 Never Enough 212
Chapter 27 God's Favorites 216
Chapter 28 Improper Focus 224

PART FIVE: Know and Believe

Chapter 29 Nothing More than Feelings. 231
Chapter 30 Behold 234
Chapter 31 Satisfied God 241
Chapter 32 God is Love 254
Chapter 33 Our First Love 275
Chapter 34 Love in Action 281
Chapter 35 Know and Believe 298

Epilogue 303
About the Author 305
Books by C. D. Hildebrand 306
Communications 308
Studies in Grace and Faith 308

This Book is for You If

This book is for you if:

You feel confident of God's love for you, and you want to learn more about it.

You once knew the love of God for you, but for reasons you cannot identify, the awareness of His love for you seems a distant memory.

You used to daily experience the presence of God, but now He seems far away.

You are doing all you think you are supposed to do to please God, but you aren't certain that you do.

You've tried all the formulas for getting close to God but instead of getting closer, He seems farther away.

You want nothing to do with the religion of Christianity, but you still love Jesus.

You feel God has set you aside when it comes to ministry for no reason you can identify.

Know and Believe

You know that God loves you, but you sense He is disappointed and ashamed of you because you don't meet the "Christian" standards of success in life and ministry.

You often wake up or go to bed thinking that God is displeased with you.

You've been beaten down in life by overwhelming experiences and by people who should have loved you but didn't.

You remember the joy and love you felt the hour you first believed in Jesus, but most of what you've learned since then has, in subtle ways, minimized His love for you.

You sometimes find yourself unemotional when the topic of God's love is taught, and you are wondering what is wrong with you.

You know people who need to know and believe that God loves them, and you're looking for a book that might help.

You are ready to begin a lifetime journey toward rediscovering God's beautiful, astounding, and precious love for you.

Foreword

As a pastor, author and Christian leader, it is humbling - almost embarrassing - to admit how often I need to re-focus my mind upon the stunning depths of God's love for me. In my own battle against perfectionism, legalism and a shame-based self-image that was formed in my early childhood, I need companions in life like Cathy Hildebrand, whose teachings and writings always bring me back to the absolute unconditionality of my Heavenly Father's love for me.

Know and Believe is a book I anticipate turning to many times as a trustworthy guide when the persistent voices of the world, the flesh and the enemy seek to cloud my assurance of amazing grace. Please consider reading this book and sharing it with others. You will be glad you did!

Jeremy White
Pastor of Valley Church, Vacaville, California
Author of The Gospel Uncut: Learning to Rest in the
Grace of God
Co-Author of 40 Days of Renewal: A Journey toward Freedom
Husband, father, friend

Dear Reader,

How smart of you to read this book! Who doesn't love a good love story? And this book eloquently and deliberately displays the best love story of all! God's love for us! How magnificent to reflect on His tremendous love for me and you. What a fantastic way to spend our time.

Speaking of time, the author, my mom, has this great thing she does with the clock. Whenever it tells a cool time like 1:23 or 3:33 or 4:56, she stops and remembers how much God loves her. This book, too, is a great and timely reminder of how much God loves us! I hope you are encouraged in His love through reading it...I was!

Joella Haley
Lover of Jesus, wife to Ben, mommy to Joel, Nathan, Annie, Alice, and Sam, friend to all and
Someone who knows whose daughter she is

I read this book in the midst of one of the most challenging times of my life. Both our sons have battled mental illness since they were seven years old and continue to battle it at the ages of 22 and 25. It's been a long journey where doubts have crept in about God's goodness.

As I began reading this book, I thought, "I *know* this stuff."

Then, I heard the gentle voice of my loving Father saying, "Yes, you do; however, you need new faith and this reminder to again *believe* it."

Then I looked at the title, which I hadn't paid attention to—Know AND Believe. I had to chuckle. A believer for over 35 years, and I still need a reminder and new faith to believe Him.

Cathy writes with a tender heart, considering all walks of life and the common challenges that we share as human beings. I believe it will encourage and challenge all who read it to question what they know and believe and encourage them to Know AND Believe the truth about our God who is loving, patient, kind, good, faithful, gentle, and amazingly GOOD despite our crushing circumstances.

This book has breathed life back into my soul by giving me new faith to believe Him though life is still out of control. It's given me courage and permission to again believe that His love for my family and for me is better than I could ever ask or imagine. This is a priceless gift. May you receive it and pass it on.

Mary Saip
Independent Consultant & Director for the Pampered Chef ®
Wife and mother
Treasured friend

The very same peace and reassurance that I receive from Jesus when I speak to Him about things that concern me is what I am receiving as I read this truth-telling book. I really appreciate how the author lovingly approaches the many misconceptions about God that cause us to doubt His love using scripture after scripture that are within context.

The words are soothing and healing. As Jesus stated, "You will know the truth and the truth will set you free." Be free to grow in the knowledge of the great love with which He loves us.

Suzanne Markey
Content Editor and sweet friend

I love reading books about God's grace and love for us. There are a lot of great books and many excellent authors writing about this, and I always enjoy the unique and various ways in which this message is presented. My favorite of these books are the ones authored by C. D. Hildebrand.

Her previous two books are a great source of encouragement and inspiration to me, and this latest one no less so. I learned a great deal as I read Know and Believe but I never felt as if I was being taught, and I guess that's one of the things I love best about Cathy's approach.

Indeed, she is teaching, but she does so in a manner that doesn't make you feel like you're learning in a classroom. Instead, you feel like you're sitting on the porch, perhaps drinking from a pitcher of refreshing iced tea, and she is simply sharing her knowledge of this great God who gives to us His amazing grace and unconditional love. So personal is her telling, you can tell she has this relationship with Him herself, and likewise in her sharing, it's obvious she really wants us to enjoy that same relationship with Him as well.

Early on in the book, I had the wonderful experience of recalling the moment when I first knew and believed in God and experienced His grace and love for me. Cathy shares these kinds of moments in her own life with us, and in doing so reminds us of our own, making for a wonderful reading experience. I also enjoy the way in which she lovingly and carefully "unteaches" believers things we've been wrongly taught all our lives.

I very highly recommend <u>Know and Believe</u> to you. It's one that you will enjoy the first time and many times more, one you will want to share with others—this very good news of God's grace and love for us, and it's one that will change your life and make you more appreciative of that change. It will encourage you, inspire you, and most of all, either introduce you to or remind you of our God who gives us His grace and love.

Mark Cermak
Believer in Jesus Christ
One grateful for the grace and love of God
Grammar and Content Editor

Acknowledgements

*G*od's love was first shown to me through my mother who, with limited resources, dedicated her life to raising me every day the best she knew how and whose love I never once doubted. My life would not be where it is today without her.

I am so thankful God graciously brought David Hildebrand into my life. God knew I had only a negative reference when it came to selecting a husband. I didn't know what I wanted, only what I didn't. He remains my best and dearest friend who demonstrates His love for me in word and deed every day. Thank-you, David, for always being my first editor which has been key to keeping me from embarrassing myself.

Our children, Christina, Joella, and Tim, and their wonderful spouses Eric, Ben, and Amanda continue to amaze me as I witness the grace and love of God in their lives. Their examples of faith encourage me and countless others, and I treasure our relationships deeply.

When life gets dull as it sometimes does, our grandchildren can completely pull me out of any negative thinking. I love witnessing their energy, genuine personalities, and accomplishments. Each day they give me ten very good reasons to live the longest and healthiest life possible and to keep sharing the GOOD news about GOOD things from our GOOD God. Those ten reasons are Emma, Levi, Joel, Grace, Nathan, Amy, Annie, Josh, Alice and Sam.

My heart fills with joy as I remember my dear friends who are my most faithful cheerleaders. We share in our life struggles, rejoice together when things go well, and enrich each other's lives with so much love—to Linda and Janet and many others who are living this grace and faith life and who encourage me constantly, thank-you so much for being part of this journey.

To those who previewed this work before it was published, there are not enough words to express how appreciated you are. This book would not be what it is without your input.

Thank-you, Mary, for your "where the rubber meets the road" perspective of my writings that you give due to the multiple ways these truths have been challenged in your life. Yet you remain steadfast in His great love for you which is an inspiration, not only to me, but to everyone who knows you.

Jeremy, your input as a pastor who teaches the gospel of the grace of God, is so important. You are able to read with the perspective of someone who deals with people on a day-to-day basis in the "real" world, and yet you also allow your heart to be touched personally by His love. You give me confidence that what I'm writing is not only doctrinally sound but practical. Thank-you so much.

I'm grateful for my cousin, Nancy, who reads my books as if to find hidden treasure and who dialogs with my writings by scribbling her thoughts throughout and then shares those with me with such love. Your English teacher skills, your love, and your enthusiasm are deeply cherished.

To Mark, whom we've never met, but who has been an instrumental help on my last two books as far as grammar is concerned, and his priceless way of making me think my books are his favorites, Brother, you are awesome.

David Graybiel, not only does your partnership in ministry mean so much to David and me, but your perspective as someone who studied false doctrine in detail is a significant resource. I know you will tell me if I ever go off into extra-Biblical teachings. Please know that you and your dear wife, Sharon, are deeply loved and appreciated by both of us.

Bruce, thanks for your input and helping me keep my historical facts straight. We appreciate your friendship and Sandy's. To all of you who encouraged me personally and on social media while I was composing and endlessly editing these pages, thank-you once again for your friendship and your partnership in sharing the good news of God's amazing grace with His beloved children.

I thank my God upon every remembrance of you
⁴ always in every prayer of mine making request for you all
with joy, ⁵ for your fellowship in the gospel from the first day
until now, ⁶ being confident of this very thing, that He who
has begun a good work in you will complete it until the day
of Jesus Christ; ⁷ just as it is right for me to think this of you
all, because I have you in my heart, inasmuch as both in my
chains and in the defense and confirmation of the gospel, you
all are partakers with me of grace. ⁸ For God is my witness,
how greatly I long for you all with the affection of Jesus Christ.
⁹ And this I pray, that your love may abound still more and
more in knowledge and all discernment, ¹⁰ that you may
approve the things that are excellent, that you may be sincere and without offense till the day of Christ, ¹¹ being filled
with the fruits of righteousness which are by Jesus Christ, to
the glory and praise of God.

Philippians 1:3-11

Prologue

While writing my first book[1], I hoped there would be another eventually, but after what seemed like endless editing, I was pretty sure I never *wanted* to go through that process again. Plus, it didn't seem possible there was anything else for me to say.

It was only as I later began to teach a series on the topic of how to overcome those areas in our lives that seem to be unconquerable, that it became clear my second book would take a new look at the topic of faith in God's grace. While composing my second book[2], it was surprising to me that the idea for the third book (the one you hold in your hands) came into focus so soon. It was in my heart almost the entire time I was writing the second book.

After nearly finishing the final draft for the second book, I sensed there was more to say, and I wrote in the Epilogue:

> *Last night, as I sat in the dark, so I could*
> *see the stars in the late-night sky through the*
> *window of my office, I asked the Lord if there*

---

[1] Are We Preaching "Another" Gospel, a 31 Day Journey toward Rediscovering the Gospel of the Grace of God

[2] Overcoming the Overwhelming, A 40 Day Journey toward Rediscovering Faith in God

was anything else He wanted me to add to my book.

Almost instantly, the thought came to me, "Remind them that I love them," and I began weeping tears of joy.

Dear Friends, God loves you. He really does. Oh, if we could only understand this one thrilling and profound truth, all fear and doubt would cease! "In every high and stormy gale" Jesus loves you.

Please carefully consider the glorious certainty of how perfectly you are adored by your God. Let Him love you. You don't have to feel anything; simply believe.

*And we have known and believed
the love God has for us.
God is love,
and he who abides in love
abides in God, and God in him.*

1 John 4:16

May this book lay solid foundations for your own glorious lifetime journey of rediscovering how profoundly and sincerely God loves you, and may you be set free forever from any doubt of this glorious truth.

**God's unconditional love for us
❧ is the most important and precious treasure ☙
we as Christians possess.**

Introduction

*W*hile contemplating the desire to write about the vastness of God's love for us, I was faced with my immense
inability to do so. Due to the devastating teachings received
as a young adult that caused me to doubt God's love for me,
and even after many years of understanding the good news
of God's grace, it was still difficult for me to truly experience
God's love while it seemed so many others were so sweetly
touched by it. Since my husband is one of those people, I initially asked him if he would co-author this book; and for a year,
it seemed the only possible way to communicate God's love
to others would be if he helped me, since he was more clearly
moved by how deeply God loved him.

Yet as the time was drawing near for me to begin this work,
there came a certain encouragement from God to write it
myself. After conferring with David, he whole-heartedly agreed.
It was at that moment of him once again setting me free to fly
that what had been developing in my heart for so long was
able to be birthed, and in the space of one morning, this entire
book was outlined.

To my amazement, the more thought I've given to this, that
someone who has grappled so greatly with truly believing God
loves her would write a book about His love for us, the more
sense it makes. Surely there are others who experience these
insecurities. Perhaps those who struggle similarly will find it
easier to be encouraged by someone like myself who has
made significant progress in this area of knowing and believing

she is loved by her God and who continues a lifetime journey toward rediscovering His love for her.

Even if someone were to know all there is to know about God's love and be able to experience it fully, it is doubtful he could communicate it in one lifetime. So expansive is His love for us that perhaps we will still be exploring it throughout eternity.

That lovely thought delights my heart and causes me to rest. Perhaps it is wonderful enough to simply explore and learn of His love for us instead of thinking we need to understand it all at once. Maybe the journey toward discovering His love is part of His very plan of loving us. Just that idea fills my spirit with joy and hope.

As I begin to type the first pages of this work, tears fill my eyes because I sense God is giving me confidence, and He will help me communicate what He is teaching the body of Christ—that He will use this book to encourage others to know and believe the love God has for them. The pressure to expound on every aspect of His love for us has been replaced by a peaceful and sincere desire to simply set you on your own path of discovering again and again how deeply your God loves you.

> *Could we with ink the ocean fill,*
> *And were the skies of parchment made,*
> *Were every stalk on earth a quill,*
> *And every man a scribe by trade;*
> *To write the love of God above*
> *Would drain the ocean dry;*
> *Nor could the scroll contain the whole,*
> *Though stretched from sky to sky.*
> *Oh, love of God, how rich and pure!*
> *How measureless and strong!*
> *It shall forevermore endure—*
> *The saints' and angels' song.*[3]

---

[3] *"Oh, Love of God," Frederick Martin Lehman | Meir Ben Isaac Nehorai, © Words: Public Domain, Music: Public Domain*

Whoever confesses that Jesus is the Son of God,
God abides in him,
and he abides in God.
And we have known and believed
the love that God has for us.
God is love,
and he who abides in love abides in God,
and God in him.

1 John 4:15-16

God Loves You

God loves you.
That is something you cannot change.
He loves you
As you are
Where you are
No matter what you are doing.

He loves you
Even if you don't love Him
Even if you don't believe in Him
Even if you don't love yourself.

His love for you is E N O R M O U S.

His love for you is not based on how successful you are.
His love is not withheld from you if you are a failure.
He loves you, even if no one else on earth loves you.

He loves you because He created you.
He loves you because He is love.
Loving is who He is, and loving is what He does.
He simply and completely loves you.

God has some things to say to you.
"You are not alone.
I see you.
I know you.
I love you.
I am not mad at you.
I am not holding your faults against you."

Know and Believe

Can you hear Him speaking to you?
He is saying, "Come to Me and I will give you rest."
You might ask, "How?"
God says, "Believe in my Son, Jesus."
He came to earth, gave His life for you,
rose from the dead and lives forevermore.

Do you believe this?
If you do, there is one more thing for you to do.
Believe in Him as the Lord.
You might say, "Well, I don't."
God already knows this, and yet He still loves you
Because He loves you even if you don't believe in Him
Even if you don't love Him back.

No matter who or what may have hurt you
No matter whom you may have hurt
He cares and wants to help you.
He wants to heal your pain and use you to help others.
Sound impossible?
Nothing is impossible for Him.

If you don't believe in Him, He already knows.
If you ask Him,
He will open your eyes to see.

If you believe in Him but feel insecure
about His love for you—
If you think His love for you
is conditional on what you do and don't do,
He wants to show you that isn't true.
If you ask Him,
He will help you to know and believe
The love He has for you
And set you free
From every thought and deed
That causes you to doubt His super-abundant affection.

No matter how you feel right now, God loves you.
He wants to give you His life.
Reach out to Him
because He's reaching out to you.[4]

---

[4] "God Loves You," a poem by C. D. Hildebrand

PART 1

His Love on Display

Chapter 1

THE JOURNEY HOME

*M*y mother was a "preacher's kid" during a time when legalisms included not reading the comics and only being allowed to wear clear fingernail polish on Sundays. She was surrounded by many unreasonable religious standards and expectations God never intended for His people, along with the crushing pressure to be the picture perfect eldest preacher's daughter. The good news about this, from my perspective, is while she lived under a profusion of law and legalism, this motivated her to raise me with an abundance of love and grace.

So it was, the first seven years of my life. God's love surrounded me, and I could feel it so intensely. My earliest memories are of singing songs about Jesus' love for me in the backseat of our car and sensing God's love with all my being.

> *Jesus love me; this I know*
> *For the Bible tells me so.*
> *Little ones to Him belong.*
> *They are weak, but He is strong.*
>
> *Yes, Jesus loves me.*
> *Yes, Jesus loves me.*
> *Yes, Jesus loves me.*
> *The Bible tells me so.*[5]

---

[5] "Jesus Loves Me", William B. Bradbury, 1862, Public Domain

The people of our church communicated God's love for my mom, my brother, and me through many kindnesses toward us. The pastors' family often invited us to their home to visit with their children and eat with them. When we had to leave that church to go live with my grandparents over 1,000 miles away, I remember a particular adult in the congregation whose eyes filled with tears when he discovered we were leaving. How deeply that love was felt by a little girl who just lost her daddy to divorce.

The next church we attended would have been a frightening experience if it hadn't been that most of my twelve cousins attended the same church which meant I got to see them almost every Sunday. The pain of divorce and loss of our loving church community was softened considerably by having aunts, uncles, and cousins in my life.

One of the positive things that happened there was that in children's church we did a lot of Bible verse memorization which helped me later in life. It was also at this church where I got down on my knees in the church pew without anyone's knowledge, while the grownups were at the altar, and formally asked Jesus to come into my heart. (He was probably already there because I sincerely believed in Him.) The adults were singing, "Into My Heart," so I prayed, "Jesus, please come into *my* heart."

However, somewhere along the line, while attending this church, my concept of what it meant to be a Christian was changed from simply *believing* in Jesus and His love for me to focusing on *not sinning* in order to be a "good" Christian. In my mind, refraining from sinning became the proof one was a Christian. This gradually produced a distance in my relationship with God, and that wonderful unconditional love I'd known seemed to dwindle a bit, though I never completely stopped believing in Him.

At a young age, I began writing my thoughts about God.

I close my eyes to say a prayer
And tell the Lord how much I care.
Although I cannot see His face,

He's standing there with all His grace.

He knows where I am
And what lies ahead
What I'm feeling and doing
And what's in my head.

He knows about
The hurts I feel
And understands
They are very real.

When I feel lost
And all alone
God leads me on
Won't let me roam

And I know He will be here
Until the end of time
To help with all of these
Troubles of mine

Even though I think
That I might die
I know He's here
Right by my side.[6]

Paul wrote, "The power of sin is the law," and this came true in my life just a couple years after composing this poem. A young woman who never desired to sin, began to sin and at some point stopped calling herself a Christian because she didn't want to be a hypocrite. What was happening was law was strengthening sin in my life. It just automatically happened

---

[6] "I Close My Eyes to Say a Prayer," a poem by C. D. Hildebrand, 1969, age 15

to me when I began basing my right-standing before God on whether or not I sinned (1 Corinthians 15:56).[7]

I'll spare you the prodigal daughter story here and skip ahead to when I reawakened to God's love for me. I'd prayed, "God, if You exist, please show me," fully fearing that if He did indeed exist, He might strike me with a bolt of lightning for being so impertinent by questioning His existence.

Instead, from within my heart, the peaceful thought came to me, "If you don't believe in Me, why are you talking to Me?"

For someone majoring in psychology, the idea that God was communicating with me was unsettling. Perhaps psychiatric care was in order. On the other hand, if God *was* talking to me—well, what an awestriking possibility, and while I tried to pretend that I could be making it all up, I was in wonder of the reality I could not deny—God was *speaking* to me.

Over the next few days, it was as if my eyes were opened to a deeper appreciation for the beauty of nature that surrounded me. Each time I would admire an aspect of it, the question would come to me, "Evolution, Cathy?" as if to challenge my developing opinion that everything gradually came into existence (instead of being created). In my Zoology class while dissecting an earthworm, instead of nodding in agreement with the idea that animal life gradually became more complex over time, I stared in amazement at the intricacies of it all.

"Evolution, Cathy?" Each time that question came into my heart, I became increasingly convinced that not only was evolution an absurd belief, but that God, yes, God was *talking* to me! He was showing me through the things He made that He existed.

Romans 1:19-20
What may be known of God is manifest in them,

---

[7] Parents, it is very important to talk to your children about this over the years. You might not know what they are being taught by others in church. Make sure they understand we are right with God by faith in Jesus, and NOT by not sinning.

for God has shown it to them. *20 For since the creation of the world His invisible attributes are clearly seen, being understood by the things that are made, even His eternal power and Godhead, so that they are without excuse.*

Not wanting to jump to conclusions about God and determined to keep an open mind as to which direction I should head next, I asked Him, "God, You have shown me that You exist, but now what?"

What I was wondering was which religion was the right way to go. I did not want to automatically assume that Jesus was the right way just because that was what I'd been taught all my life. As many others of my contemporaries were doing, it seemed to be my time to set out on a journey of finding the truth for myself.

So, my search began that moment. Wondering where to start, I remembered the Bible that was in my desk. I would start my long search for truth with the book I had on hand.

"God, here's my Bible. I'm going to read it, but You'll have to explain it to me. I want to know if Jesus is your Son."

Hey, God, here's my prayer[8]
And I do it truthfully.
I know that I can't con You, God
'Cause through me You can see.
Well, quite frankly, I doubt You're up there.
Though sometimes I think You are.
And though I might be praying to the walls,
I want You to know this is hard.

Suddenly, it occurred to me,
Hey, I'm usually not so vain,
But in hope that He was listening to me
I was praying just the same.

---

8 "Hey, God, Here's My Prayer", a song by C. D. Hildebrand written shortly after her return home, circa March 1974.

37

> *And if I didn't believe it at all*
> *I wouldn't waste my time*
> *Reaching out to Someone out there*
> *I didn't think I would find.*
>
> *So, I prayed, "God's here's Your Bible,*
> *"I'm going to read it now,*
> *"But You're gonna have to explain it to me*
> *"'Cause I've tried and I don't know how."*

With the most open mind possible, I opened to the book of Matthew and began to read. In only a few verses, I came upon the scene in which John was baptizing Jesus when a voice came from heaven saying, "This is my beloved Son in whom I am well pleased."[9]

> *And as I began to read those words[10]*
> *They opened them up to me*
> *Like a light shining down from heaven above*
> *Allowing me to see.*

This one verse started this prodigal daughter on her journey back home. It was almost as if it was highlighted with light, and it became clear without one doubt that God was answering my question. I began to cry as I again had to acknowledge that God was conversing with me. Yes, Jesus is His Son. My search for the truth was already done.

Over the next weeks, between attending classes at the university, reading the New Testament became my focus. As a teenager, I'd read most of the New Testament, but it was more alive to me than ever before, and it was obvious God was speaking to me through it and bringing me to a place of decision. It felt as if I was straddling a fence with one foot in the

---

[9] Just to clarify, that is what is recorded in Matthew. I did not hear a voice from heaven.

[10] The song continues.

world and one foot in the kingdom of God. There was a decision to be made. Would I respond to this truth or walk away?

As the days continued, a verse memorized in children's
church kept coming to my mind, though not completely, "If you
confess Jesus, you will be saved."[11] Though I was speaking to
anyone who would listen to me about "God," it became obvious
that I was not verbally attributing the changes that were happening in me to "Jesus."

One evening, a friend of mine came to say hello while I
was sitting at a table studying in the student union. Poor fellow!
Did he ever get an earful while I talked incessantly about "God"
this and "God" that—and each time I said "God," there was
an acute awareness that I was purposely not saying "Jesus."

Finally, my friend asked me, "What is going on with you?
You seem like you've changed."

I knew this was my moment to "confess Jesus." I thought
about the decision I was going to make. From deep inside I
prayed, "God, I don't know what You want from my life, but
whatever it is, I trust You will help me."

Then I looked at my friend who was patiently waiting for my
reply and answered, "It's the love of Jesus Christ." Instantly,
I was "home" with my Father sensing His love and welcome
intensely.

I nearly grabbed my friend, and said, "Did you hear what I
said? It's the love of Jesus Christ!"

From that moment, the thrill and amazement of God's
love for me once again filled my heart. Certainly the angels
in heaven were rejoicing. I thought I could fly from table to
table, though I had enough sense not to try. Then I became
suddenly aware I was missing my brothers and sisters to welcome me home, and by the next Sunday this young woman
who said she would never go to church again (because of all
the churchgoing hypocrites I'd known), was in church praising
God. It amazes me that with only a child's knowledge of the
Bible, I was able to articulate what was happening to me. The
LOVE of Jesus Christ was changing me. Even as I recall that

---

[11] Romans 10:9-10

moment, my eyes fill with tears. I sensed so profoundly the Father's pleasure and delight and knew without a doubt I was home with Him.

"Now, I thank the Lord for saving me.[12]
I thank Him for His light
I give Him all of my everything
In faith He knows what's right.
And I give Him all my sorrows
That He always turns to joy.
I give Him my tomorrows.
I give Him my right now.

Thank-You, Lord for saving me.
Thank-You for your light.
I give you all of my everything
In faith you know what's right.

Luke 15:22-24 (personalized)
"But the father said to his servants, 'Bring out the best robe and put it on her, and put a ring on her hand and sandals on her feet. [23] *And bring the fatted calf here and kill it, and let us eat and be merry;* [24] *for this my daughter was dead and is alive again; she was lost and is found.' And they began to be merry."*

Inside Out, Upside Down, and Backward

There was quite a bit of dread in my mind on the way to church with my new friends because I had no idea what kind of church it would be. Perhaps it would be one of those dreaded cults about which my grandmother warned me as a teenager. As we approached the facility, I saw the church sign with the same name as the church in which I'd grown up, and I felt a certain relief.

---

[12] The previously mentioned song continues and concludes.

As we entered the sanctuary, people were already singing praises to God. Not yet remembering I was a believer since childhood, and not then understanding that what had just happened to me was actually the story of a prodigal daughter coming home, I turned to the girl who had come with me and said, "I think I'm a baby Christian." Robin threw her arms around me and rejoiced with me. It was what I'd been missing, a welcome home. Though I didn't raise my hands as it seemed everyone else was doing, I began to sing the songs of joy which filled that place.

"That place" was not a *normal* church and nothing like my teenage church. Just a couple years prior, the very traditional attendees had opened their doors to some very suspicious characters with long hair and bell-bottom jeans who had come to Jesus out of the hippie lifestyle. MANY others had followed. The room was replete with relatively new Christians overflowing with the love of God and love for each other. It was a joyful place people *wanted* to be.

In fact, "wanted" became a way of life born out of knowing God's love for me. I *wanted* to go to church at every opportunity because I *wanted* to learn. I *wanted* to worship, to teach Sunday School, to sing in the choir, to share Jesus at our local Christian coffee house, to give generously, and to read my Bible. Prayer was as natural as breathing. I *wanted* to share this joy with my friends, even though most of them thought I'd clearly gone over the deep end. Giving up my wayward lifestyle was easy. Nothing compared to the knowledge that God loved me which caused me to flourish as I responded daily to His love. It seemed to surround me continually and as intensely as I'd known as a young girl.

During this joyous time, a close friendship developed with a young man who was living in the same "wanted" zone, and very soon we both *wanted* to marry each other. David and I *wanted* to be parents, and even though it was difficult at first, we parented with joy because we loved our children. When our church started a Bible school, we both *wanted* to attend. We both *wanted* to become licensed ministers and dedicate the rest of our lives to serving God. When asked by our pastors if

David would like to be the college minister and then the youth pastor, we both *wanted* to do that, too. We *wanted* to be "pillars in the house of our God."

**But—somewhere along the line,
our walk with God was turned inside out,
upside down, and backward.**

Whereas previously prayer was something we did b*ecause* we had perfect fellowship with God, we began to view prayer as a *means by which* we entered His presence. All the things we'd been doing out of love became "disciplines"—requirements meant to *obtain* what we'd already been given in Christ. Does this sound familiar?

We *wanted* to please God, so we looked to our leaders to show us *how* to please God. The problem was, our leaders were taught the same errors—that righteousness, holiness, closeness, and power were something we *obtained* via spiritual disciplines. We were like lonesome desperate monks beating ourselves to somehow reach communion with God—a communion we already had.

So, in the throes of self-effort, we gradually and very painfully fell from grace—not into sin, but into a miserable state of existence described by Paul as being estranged from Christ.

Galatians 5:4
You have become estranged from Christ, you who attempt to be <u>justified by law</u>; you have fallen from grace.

The above translation of this verse misses the deeper meaning. "Estranged" seems to imply that there is a break in relationship. Yet He promised to never leave us or forsake us. We don't become unsaved when we begin to seek to be made righteous by our works (laws). What happens is we are estranged from His power.

The KJV captures the meaning a little better. It reads, "Christ is become of no effect unto you." The word for "estranged" in the Greek is **kartageo** and means "to render entirely idle (useless), to become of no (none, without) effect," says Strong's Concordance. Thayer's Definition is even more revealing.

1) to render idle, unemployed, inactivate, inoperative
1a) to cause a person or thing to have no further efficiency
1b) to deprive of force, influence, power

As we sought to obtain an improved relationship with God through our own efforts, we actually ended up with the exact opposite. God seemed farther away, not closer, and we were uncertain as to whether He loved us which was the most horrible thing we experienced.

When believers begin to shift from being justified by grace through faith to being justified by law through works, they gradually become deprived of Christ's power. For us, it was such a gradual strangulation that we didn't perceive it at first. We just felt wretched and couldn't explain why. For some, this eventually led to sinning. For us, it just led to misery and perplexity.

From our perspectives, we were pretty much doing all God had supposedly asked us to do, and we were willing to do more, but couldn't figure out what "more" He wanted. We lived with the nagging sense that God was far away and that He didn't love us, even though we knew from Scripture this was not true.

Thankfully, God opened our eyes to see that we had taken a wrong turn in our beliefs, and He lovingly brought us back, away from attempting to accomplish what Jesus had already done. What a joy it was to discover once again that we did not need to enter His presence because His presence had entered us. Holiness and righteousness were gifts, not something that needed to be obtained or improved. How happily we returned to our first love—His love for us.

So, in this first chapter of our lifetime journey toward rediscovering God's love for us, let us carefully examine our hearts. Are we living a life in *response* to His grace or are we *trying to obtain* His favor? Do we do what we do *because* He loves us or *so that* He will love us? Once we get our focus off our own efforts and begin to realize what God accomplished *for* us in Christ, we will no longer be estranged and will once again benefit from His power and know His love.

**⬥ God loves us too much
to let us be content with self-effort. ⬥**

*Now may the God of peace **Himself** sanctify you completely;
and may your whole spirit, soul, and body
be **preserved** blameless
at the coming of our Lord Jesus Christ.*
[24] ***He who calls you is faithful, who also will do it****.*

1 Thessalonians 5:23-24

Beginning the Journey

At the end of each chapter of this book, there are a few questions and/or further comments. They are included because many readers ask if there are study guides for my books. Hopefully, these will be helpful. They are not a review or test of the material discussed in the chapters, but rather designed to help you analyze, personalize, or discuss the ideas presented. Feel free to interact with them as you see fit.

1.   What do you hope to discover as you begin your journey toward knowing and believing the love God has for you?

2.   Does the testimony above sound familiar to you?

3.   If you'd like, describe your current thinking concerning God's love for you.

Chapter 2

CREATION AND THE FALL

It didn't "just happen" or fall into place
The minuteness of earth, the vastness of space.
It didn't "just happen".
There's no way that it could,
But a loving Designer planned that it would.

It didn't "just happen", the moon in the sky
The sun and the stars, and I'll tell you why.
There's far too much beauty
And order involved.
It didn't "just happen" nor did it evolve.

People are searching for answers to why
There's so much beauty in earth and the sky
Their eyes have been blinded
They don't want to see
That a loving Creator caused them to be.[13]

Since the beginning of time, God's love has been evident, but often it is missed when scriptures are twisted to present a picture of a God who is constantly angry. Yet even before He created man, God tenderly crafted the perfect dwelling place, with the sun to give life and the moon and stars to give

---

[13] "It Didn't Just Happen", first half of a song by C. D. Hildebrand, 1982

rest. He supplied them with air to breathe and water to drink. He provided plentiful and delicious food to nourish and enjoy. Everything God lovingly created was "good." It was orderly and beautiful beyond compare and continues to speak of His love.

Psalm 19:1-4
The heavens declare the glory of God;
And the firmament shows His handiwork.
² Day unto day utters speech,
And night unto night reveals knowledge.
³ There is no speech nor language
Where their voice is not heard.
⁴ Their line has gone out through all the earth,
And their words to the end of the world.

When you think of God during the six days of creation, how do you picture Him? Do you see Him matter-of-factly speaking creation into being with miraculous power but with almost no sentiment? That is how I used to envision God. I was wrong. God created everything with great love. He delighted in His work and cared for His creation.

When God *lovingly* created Adam from the dust of the earth, He endowed him with reason, creativity, and spiritual life. He blessed him with the ability to see a bountiful spectrum of color and to enjoy what he would taste. He gave him the gift of speech so that He could communicate, and even though God created Adam to have fellowship with Him, God knew that Adam would need human companionship, too.

Genesis 2:20-25
So Adam gave names to all cattle, to the birds
of the air, and to every beast of the field. But for
Adam there was not found a helper comparable
to him.
²¹ And the Lord God caused a deep sleep to
fall on Adam, and he slept; and He took one
of his ribs and closed up the flesh in its place.
²² Then the rib which the Lord God had taken

from man He made into a woman, and He
brought her to the man.
²³ *And Adam said:*
"This is now bone of my bones
And flesh of my flesh;
She shall be called Woman,
Because she was taken out of Man."
²⁴ *Therefore a man shall leave his father and*
mother and be joined to his wife, and they shall
become one flesh. ²⁵ *And they were both naked,*
the man and his wife, and were not ashamed.

From Adam's own body, God *lovingly* crafted Eve. She was similar to him, but also different in ways that would bring them both joy. He granted them the ability to choose and gave them dominion over all the living things on the earth, crowning them above all the animals by creating them in His own image. After His creation was finished, God was pleased with what He made and declared it to be "*very* good."

We don't know exactly how God communicated with Adam and Eve, only that He did. There was no wondering about what His will was for they walked and talked with God. No one knows how long it was before the serpent challenged God's love for Adam and Eve. "Hath God said?" put in doubt God's words and His will for them. It brought about a shady perspective of the One who had created them and provided for their every need by accusing God of withholding from them knowledge and enlightenment. By demeaning God's goodness and claiming He lied to them about what would happen if they ate of the forbidden tree, Adam and Eve believed the serpent more than they believed God, and even with the death penalty hanging over their heads, they partook of the Tree of the Knowledge of Good and Evil, taking all of mankind with them into spiritual darkness (Rom. 5:17-19).

Thankfully, because God loved Adam and Eve, He already had a plan to save them from the consequences of their sin. We know this because it is written that Jesus was "slain *before* the foundations of the earth" (Rev. 13:8). God did not "plan" for

Adam and Eve to fall. He didn't "allow" them to fall. He simply knew in advance that they would and provided a way that they could one day be restored to spiritual life with God.

God sent the ones He loved out of the garden because He did not want them to partake of the Tree of Life and remain in their sinful state forever. Their sin had grave consequences, but we see the tenderness of God still in action as He protected them from a worse fate than they'd already brought upon themselves.

Then the Lord God said, "Behold, the man has become like one of Us, to know good and evil. And now, lest he put out his hand and take also of the tree of life, and eat, and live forever"— [23] therefore the Lord God sent him out of the garden of Eden to till the ground from which he was taken.

Genesis 3:22-23

Continuing the Journey

1. Do you remember a situation in which your belief in God's love for you was challenged by bringing God's good character into question? Please record or share your experience.

2. When Adam and Eve sinned, God promised a Redeemer for humanity. That Redeemer, of course, was Jesus. Whereas, Adam and Eve were punished for their sin, we will not come into judgment for ours (John 5:24). How can knowing this positively affect our relationship with God?

Chapter 3

GOD'S HEART OF LOVE

*I*t is commonly taught that when Adam and Eve sinned they were separated from fellowship with God because, "God cannot look upon sin," and, "Sin separates us from God." Both of these statements are untrue.

Adam and Eve suffered a spiritual death which was brought upon all of the human race, but instead of a separation, and immediately after the original sin, God sought them out. He saw both them and their sin. He tenderly sewed together clothing made of animal skins to cover their nakedness and to prepare them for the harsh environment they would face. Then He mercifully led them out of the garden He created so that He could prevent them from living forever in their fallen sinful condition.

He talked with Cain, too, before he killed his brother to avert the tragedy, and even though Cain ignored God's counsel and became the first murderer, God spoke with him after his horrific deed. When Cain complained that his punishment was too great, God put a mark on him *to protect him* from human reprisal.

Enoch, who was spiritually dead (as all human beings were until the resurrection of Jesus), walked with God (Col. 2:13). He wasn't born again or in any way redeemed from the fall, but he communed with the living God. So wonderful was their relationship, that God took him off the earth without experiencing death (Gen. 5:22-24).

As the centuries scrolled by, God watched as mankind became increasingly evil and violent. I used to imagine a few thousand human beings inhabiting the earth at the time of Noah, but it has been estimated by considering genealogies and the lengthy lifespan, that at the time of Noah, there may have been nearly seven billion inhabitants on the earth[14]—close to the number there are today. Consider this estimated population when reading the following passage.

> **Genesis 6:5-8 AMP**
> The LORD saw that the wickedness (depravity) of man was **great** on the earth, and that **every** imagination or intent of the thoughts of his heart were **only evil continually**. [6] The LORD regretted that He had made mankind on the earth, and He was [deeply] grieved in His heart. [7] So the LORD said, "I will destroy (annihilate) mankind whom I have created from the surface of the earth—not only man, but the animals and the crawling things and the birds of the air—because it [deeply] grieves Me [to see mankind's sin] and I regret that I have made them." [8] But Noah found favor and grace in the eyes of the LORD.

The world in which we live today is exceedingly wicked. People are hateful and increasingly violent, and evil is daily perpetrated against innocents. Men and nations plot genocide and carry it out. Daily the human race teeters and totters between peace and utter extinction. Yet as horrid as this earth is, there is no comparing it to what God witnessed at the time of Noah. Today, there are still millions of people who seek peace, who sincerely seek to love others and do good. Multiple millions believe in Jesus and are in constant communion with Him. Many nations seek to be at peace with their neighbors. In

---

[14] Those who calculate such numbers agree they could be off on their estimates. The Bible does not tell us, so we don't really know.

Noah's time, *every* intent of *everyone* was *only* evil *continually*. Can you imagine such a world today?

Imagine the danger mankind faced. We don't often think of that. God's plan was to bring a Redeemer through a baby born to a virgin (Matt. 1:23). As others have pointed out, in such a climate, there could be no such birth. There was no Savior to redeem mankind from this depraved condition, and no hope that they could last "until the fulness of time" would come (Gal. 4:4).

God's heart was broken in view of what mankind had become. It deeply grieved Him. Yet in order to save mankind, He regretfully destroyed that evil generation. Think about it, He had no other choice if we were to survive until we could be redeemed.

By faith Noah, being divinely warned of things not yet seen, moved with godly fear, prepared an ark for the saving of his household, by which he condemned the world and became heir of the righteousness which is according to faith.

Hebrews 11:7

Continuing the Journey

1.   In what ways do you envision creation? How was His love evidenced then?

2.   What was your understanding of the reasons for the Flood? Did you see it as God's way of punishing mankind or a means of saving us? How is it that the flood can be seen as an act of love?

3.   We get a glimpse of the broken heart of God when we have faithfully and sacrificially loved and given to a child,

a friend or a spouse, only to be rejected. Sometimes we contributed to the separation, but often this is not the case. Think about this, was God to blame for the behavior of the inhabitants of the earth? Did He not do everything to provide for them, and yet they rejected Him anyway? Yes, of course, let us take responsibility for anything we have done to exacerbate a relationship, but let us not take blame where it is not due. Even God doesn't force His love on us. Discuss this point if you'd like.

4. Read again the passage above (Rom. 15:18-19). When Adam sinned, judgment came to all men resulting in death. When Jesus died, He provided justification of life. By whose obedience are we made righteous, ours or His? As Christians, do we have death and condemnation or everlasting life? Are we sinners or are we righteous?

Chapter 4

UNDERSTANDING COVENANTS

*G*od does not change or evolve, nor does He need to learn or progress socially (Mal. 3:6). He did not begin as some primitive being and gradually progress to a more civilized deity. He is today who He has always been—love. This characterization of God as love was true in eternity past and will be true forevermore. Yet many develop a near-sighted, inconsistent, and fearful opinion of God that only scarcely includes love.

Contributing first to this confusion are those outside the church whose opinions about God are often invented by their own irrational conclusions based on faulty information. They unjustly malign God; that is, if they acknowledge His existence at all. They blame Him for everything including destructive weather, disease, criminal behavior, and their own personal difficulties. They demand, "If God exists, why does He allow such suffering in the world?"

Unfortunately, many within the church today also blame God for the same things, either attributing these types of tragedies to God's judgment or claiming that God uses these evil events to bring about good. No wonder people are confused about the love of God!

For those of us whose perception of God has become warped, we need to clarify and expand our understanding of God as love. To do this, it is important that we be keenly aware of God's covenantal relationships and that we are able to distinguish between them.

The Big Picture

2 Timothy 2:15 NASB
Be diligent to present yourself approved to God as a workman who does not need to be ashamed, accurately handling the word of truth.

When we study the Bible, it is important for us to "accurately handle the worth of truth."[15] This means that it is not enough to read Scripture and then quickly apply it to our lives without understanding the context of a passage. Otherwise, we can become confused about who God is and the loving relationship He wants to have with us.

Sometimes, while reading a news article, I come across the name of a location, and I have no idea where it is; so, I will do an online search to find it. Usually, the search gives me a close-up view of the city, but not much information as to where it is actually located. The remedy, of course, is to zoom out to see the whole picture. I might find that the city is in a whole different state, country, or continent. We need to do this while studying the Bible—zoom out before zooming in.

God is always love, but throughout time He dealt differently with different people based on the covenant (or lack thereof) that He had with them. Anyone who has read the entire Bible without this understanding will likely conclude that God has a personality disorder. One day He is very happy. The next, He is rip-roaring angry. In one situation, He pours out undeserved blessings. In another similar one, He delivers wrath. During certain portions of Scripture, it seems He turns a blind eye toward obvious wrong-doing, even blessing those who engaged in it. Then a few chapters later, He is denouncing every wrong deed. This has everything to do with differing covenantal relationships.

My husband absolutely adores his children and grandchildren. He would do anything for them including dying to

---

[15] Dissect correctly, rightly divide", Strongs. Some see this as dividing between the Old and New Covenant.

save them. When our children were living at home he was committed to providing for them, nurturing them, and having a close relationship. However, he did not behave this way with all the other kids in the neighborhood. He was always kind to their friends, of course, but he didn't have a father-child covenant with other people's kids. Even though our children are now adults, they have keys to our front door. No other friend of our children has a key to our house because they are not our kids.

Can you see that we behave differently with people based on our relationships with them? Do you tell everyone you know your deepest secrets? No—not even on social media. You reserve those matters closest to your heart for a trusted few.

It would have been so much easier to understand the Bible if we'd comprehended the following concept from the start. Much confusion could have been avoided.

God does not change, BUT His covenants with certain groups of people do.

That is to say, that throughout time, God made covenants with different persons and nations, and His responses to those groups has been according to the covenant He had with them. This unlocks the mysterious confusion about God's supposed impulsive and unpredictable nature.

The law of Moses declared, "Thou shalt not lie," and a guilty individual was cursed and, furthermore, considered guilty of the whole law having only broken one commandment (Js. 2:10).

For example, most agree that lying is wrong. Then why does it seem that God didn't seem to notice when Abraham lied about the identity of his wife, Sarah—twice? God never rebuked Abraham for lying or putting his wife at risk, but He did rebuke Pharaoh. In fact, Abraham came out of these situations better off financially than before (Gen. 20).

When we lack a view of the whole picture and we don't understand that God dealt differently with different ones based on the covenant He had with them, we can develop a confused view of God. Abraham was not judged for lying because there was no law yet about lying, and "where there is no law, there is no transgression," (Rom. 4:15). In fact, Abraham was never under the law of Moses.

When we understand this, we get a clearer picture of why God dealt with Abraham with considerable grace and why He dealt with Israel more severely when they were under the law. God never said to Abraham, "Your sins have separated you from your God,"[16] but He did say this to those under the Old Testament who forsook God and worshipped idols (Isa. 59:2).

More Perspective

As believers in Jesus Christ, we have more zooming out to do when it comes to distinguishing between covenants. Far too many in the church today have the concept of being under a combination of the moral law of Moses (the Old Covenant) and the New Covenant of grace.[17] Our beliefs vary from thinking that if we don't follow the Ten Commandments, we could go to hell, to the idea that if we sin, our relationship with God is damaged, and we must obtain forgiveness through confession for the purpose of restoring ourselves to right-standing and relationship with God. Sadly, this interferes with believing that God's love for us is unconditional and constant.

Though this is discussed extensively in my first book, it is important to emphasize this point. To know and believe that God loves us, it is imperative that we are convinced of this truth.

> ❧ Christians are under only one covenant, ☙
> the New Covenant,
> and the Old Covenant
> which includes the moral law, is obsolete.

---

[16] Nor does He say this to those under the New Covenant.

[17] This is commonly referred to as "mixture."

Exodus 34:28
So he was there with the Lord forty days and forty nights; he neither ate bread nor drank water. And He wrote on the tablets the words of the covenant, the Ten Commandments.[18]

2 Corinthians 3:7-11
*But if the <u>ministry of death,</u> **written and engraved on stones**, was glorious, so that the children of Israel could not look steadily at the face of Moses because of the glory of his countenance, which glory was passing away, [8] how will the <u>ministry of the Spirit</u> not be more glorious? [9] For if the <u>ministry of condemnation</u> had glory, the <u>ministry of righteousness</u> exceeds much more in glory. [10] For even what was made glorious had no glory in this respect, because of the glory that excels. [11] For if what is passing away was glorious, what remains is much more glorious.*

Hebrews 8:13
In that He says, "A new covenant," He has made the first obsolete.

Galatians 3:23-25
*But before faith came, we were kept under guard by the law, kept for the faith which would afterward be revealed. [24] Therefore the law was our tutor to bring us to Christ, that we might be justified by faith. [25] But after faith has come, **we are no longer under a tutor**.*

Romans 6:14
For sin shall not have dominion over you, for you are not under law but under grace.

Galatians 2:21
I do not set aside the grace of God; for if righteousness comes through the law, then Christ died in vain.

Focusing in Again

After we focus out to see the big picture, we have a better perception of God's character and unchanging love and are more adequately equipped to interpret Scripture. Only then

---

[18] Notice that the Ten Commandments ARE the Old Covenant.

may we focus in on Jesus and begin to see the enormity of God's love for us.

See what an incredible quality of love
the Father has shown to us,
that we would [be permitted to] be
named and called and counted
the children of God!
And so we are!

1 John 3:1 AMP

Continuing the Journey

1. As we read Genesis through Malachi, we witness time and again God's guidance of man until the coming of the promised Seed. On your journey toward rediscovering God's love, carefully observe the tender lovingkindness of God from Genesis through Malachi while considering the different covenants He had or didn't have with people. Record or share some examples that come to mind.

Chapter 5

THE LAW'S LOVING PURPOSE

One evening while teaching a series on the difference between the Old and New Covenants, I gave a multiple-choice question as an introduction for one of the lessons. It went something like this.

As New Covenant believers, the Ten Commandments are:
   a. Our moral guide.
   b. The ministry of death
   c. The ministry of condemnation
   d. Still a requirement for us to follow.
   e. a and d
   f. b and c

The look on the gentleman's face who sat on the pew in front of me was unforgettable when it was revealed the answer was f. His mouth dropped open as his eyes read the answer again with a question mark creased in his forehead. He was visibly unsettled and then looked at me wide-eyed and baffled, nearly trembling. Then I shared the following verse with the class.

> **2 Corinthians 3:5-11**
> *Not that we are sufficient of ourselves to think of anything as being from ourselves, but our sufficiency is from God, ⁶ who also made us*

> *sufficient as ministers of the new covenant, not of the letter but of the Spirit; for the letter kills, but the Spirit gives life.* ⁷ *But if the **ministry of death, written and engraved on stones**, was glorious, so that the children of Israel could not look steadily at the face of Moses because of the glory of his countenance, which glory was passing away,* ⁸ *how will the ministry of the Spirit not be more glorious?* ⁹ *For if the **ministry of condemnation** had glory, the ministry of righteousness exceeds much more in glory.* ¹⁰ *For even what was made glorious had no glory in this respect, because of the glory that excels.* ¹¹ *For if what is passing away was glorious, what remains is much more glorious.*

In Need of a Tutor

As those who now understand we are not in any way under the law of Moses, we are sometimes baffled as to why God would institute what Paul called the ministry of death and con-demnation in the first place. Some believe it never was God's intention to establish the law but rather think the law was a reaction to the people's demands that God speak to them through Moses and not to them directly. Whatever one's par-ticular view on this subject might be, Paul, who wrote most of the New Testament letters, taught that the law had a specific plan and purpose.

First, the law set a moral standard for the nation of Israel by giving them very specific instructions about every aspect of life. Those of us who put our faith in Jesus are new creations. We are free from and dead to sin (Rom. 6). The Holy Spirit guides us from *within*. The grace of God teaches us to deny worldly lusts. The Israelites did not have these blessings. They needed *external* guidance as to what was acceptable behavior. They were like young children who needed to be told what was right and wrong.

Galatians 3:19-23

*What purpose then does the law serve? It was added because of transgressions, till the Seed should come to whom the promise was made; and it was appointed through angels by the hand of a mediator. ²⁰ Now a mediator does not mediate for one only, but God is one. ²¹ Is the law then against the promises of God? Certainly not! For if there had been a law given which could have given life, truly righteousness would have been by the law. ²² But the Scripture has confined all under sin, that the promise by faith in Jesus Christ might be given to those who believe. ²³ **But before faith came, we were kept under guard by the law, kept for the faith which would afterward be revealed.***

The law was perfect but didn't give life. The Ten Commandments were necessary to guide the people until faith would come. The phrase "faith would come" refers to the covenant in which we live. We are saved and live by grace through faith in Jesus. They were blessed and not cursed by obeying the law.

It cannot be emphasized enough. Under the New Covenant we are made righteous by faith not by following the law (Gal. 2:21). We are taught by the grace of God (Ti. 2:11-12), not by the law. We are led by the Spirit of God, not the law (Rom. 8:14). This is true because when we "came to faith" in Jesus Christ, we entered into His New Covenant, and most amazingly were made new creations and are made spiritually alive. We DO NOT NEED the law to save us, teach us, or guide us!

Galatians 3:24-26

*Therefore the law was our tutor to bring us to Christ, that we might be justified by **faith**. ²⁵ **BUT after faith has come, we are NO LONGER under a tutor.** ²⁶ For you are all sons of God through **faith** in Christ Jesus.*

The law was lovingly designed to curb the growth of evil on the earth while leading man to Christ. All around them while in Egypt, the nation of Israel witnessed the continued growth of immorality and idolatry. However, God chose Israel to be set apart in order to bring forth the Seed who would die for all. Otherwise, mankind would have reverted to the same state in which it existed prior to the flood had it not been for the demands of the law.

The law's primary purpose now is to lead people to Christ, so that they might be forgiven and thus be righteousness by faith in Jesus Christ. Not until Jesus' death and resurrection could we be completely forgiven of all sin forever.

The Lawful Use of the Law

It is important to notice in Romans 7 that Paul did not say the law died in order for us to be free from it. He stated that we died to the law. In other words, the law is obviously still in existence, but we who believe in Christ are no longer under the law but rather under grace and therefore no longer under the dominion of sin.

> **Romans 7:4-6**
> *Therefore, my brethren, you also have become **dead to the law** through the body of Christ, that you may be married to another—to Him who was raised from the dead, that we should bear fruit to God. ⁵ For when we were in the flesh, the **sinful passions which were <u>aroused by the law</u>** were at work in our members to bear fruit to death. ⁶ But now we have been **delivered from the law, having died to what we were held by**, so that we should serve in the newness of the Spirit and not in the oldness of the letter.*
> **Romans 6:14**
> *For sin shall not have dominion over you, **because** you are not under law but under grace.*

If the law arouses sinful passions, would it not have been a good idea to slay it as well? Why does it go on existing if it is the ministry of death and of condemnation? It is because the law still has a lawful purpose.

> **1 Timothy 1:8-11**
> *But we know that the law is good **if one uses it lawfully**, ⁹ knowing this: that the law is **not made for a righteous person**, but for the lawless and insubordinate, for the **ungodly and for sinners**, for the unholy and profane, for murderers of fathers and murderers of mothers, for manslayers, ¹⁰ for fornicators, for sodomites, for kidnappers, for liars, for perjurers, and if there is any other thing that is contrary to sound doctrine, ¹¹ according to the glorious gospel of the blessed God which was committed to my trust.*

The only lawful use of the law today is to instruct unbelievers who are breaking the law that they need a Savior to set them free from the law's power over them. No one can make themselves righteous. They can try really hard to live a good life, but they will fall short of God's very high standards. As we quoted above, the law is a tutor to lead us to Christ. That is the only legitimate use of it. The law is not needed to teach or guide Christians. It can never make anyone righteous because righteousness is by *faith* in Jesus Christ alone.

Let me try to give some simple examples by asking these questions. Is it better for children to behave because they fear punishment and desire reward, or don't we prefer they obey because they *want* to? Both motivations result in good behavior, but only one of these are the result of a changed child.

Which marital love would you prefer to receive, a mandated love motivated by threatened punishment and promised reward or a love coming freely from the heart? The same is true of any relationship. No one wants to be obliged to be a friend to another, nor do we want to be "loved" by someone under coercion.

Many Christians today live holy and disciplined lives because they want God's love and favor and/or are afraid of His punishment. This was God's plan for those under the Old Covenant because He knew their sinful natures would tend toward unrighteousness (which is clearly demonstrated again and again), but His loving purpose of the law was to lead the nation to Christ which would result in them being changed so they would *want to* please Him out of love for Him without the need for reward or punishment.

Saving Mankind

God's goal before time began was to bring a Savior into the world. We might not understand the intricacies of God's timing, but we know His intent was to keep evil at bay until Jesus would come. He chose to do this through the children of Abraham, and though they failed many times, His law continued to guide them to the moment when Jesus would arrive and save them. All of this elaborate planning was motivated by His intense love for them and for us—for you.

*For when we were in the flesh, the sinful passions which were aroused by the law were at work in our members to bear fruit to death. ⁶ But **now we have been delivered from the law**, having died to what we were held by, so that we should serve in the newness of the Spirit and not in the oldness of the letter.*

Romans 7:5-6

Continuing the Journey

Law vs. Grace

When Jesus died on the cross, He did not say, "It is started." He said, "It is finished." Yet there are many believers who firmly believe we are saved by grace through faith, but that after we've been redeemed, we live by law through works. Jesus saved them with unconditional love, but they have come to believe His love for them now as His child, is conditional on what they do and don't do.

When studying Scripture, they make little distinction between what God said and how He related to people before the cross and how He relates to people now. This brings about confusion because the same God who said to the Children of Israel under the law, "But your iniquities have separated you from your God; and your sins have hidden His face from you, so that He will not hear," says to those under the New Covenant, "I will never leave you or forsake you—no, not ever," (Isa. 59:2,Heb.13:5).

Which is it? Is God's back turned to you with His fingers in His ears refusing to hear you or help you when you call upon Him because you are not behaving perfectly, or is He living inside of you having promised to never ever leave you? **If you think you are under the law and its blessings and curses, you will continue to struggle to know and believe God loves you**. When hardship comes your way as it does to every person on the planet, you might tend to think God is punishing you and simply accept it instead of turning to Him for deliverance.

If we do not understand that we are not under the law, we cannot fully understand grace because when we add law, any law, to grace, grace is negated.

Romans 11:6
And if by grace, then it is no longer of works; otherwise grace is no longer grace. But if it is of works, it is no longer grace; otherwise work

is no longer work.

1. As you think on these things, how might trying to live in both covenants confuse someone on the topic of God's love?

2. If the above question applies to you, what has changed (or needs to change) in your understanding of God's immense love for you since you understood you are not under any part of the law?

3. How can a pastor or teacher in the body of Christ help those who are being saved to understand the topic of this chapter? What could youth pastors do differently? What about worship leaders and Sunday School teachers?

Chapter 6

THE PROPHETS, GOSPELS, PSALMS, AND PROVERBS

Who, What, When, Where, and Why?

*F*or many years when reading the Bible, we asked ourselves, "How does this apply to me?" We wanted to get every ounce of truth from each passage so we could better please and obey God. Having a better understanding of Bible interpretation, we now realize the question we *should* have been asking ourselves was, "**Does** this apply to me?"

Think about it. Every verse of the Bible has a context. It is important to know what the context is before we can apply it personally or not. It is improper to assume that what God spoke to the nation of Israel applies to another nation, for example.

This is also true of the Gospels. Jesus was sent to minister to the Jews who were under the law, and much of what He said was directed toward them (Gal. 4:4, Mk. 1:44). Some of His teachings were general truths which could be applied to either covenant (Mt. 5:3). Other things spoke of that which was to come (Jn. 14:17). He also prophesied of judgments both immediate and eventual (Mt. 24). When we understand this, it is much easier to understand the gospels.

Would we tell someone healed of leprosy today in our churches to see the priests so they could go through the necessary ceremonies of cleansing (Lev. 13-14)? Would we tell someone that to be perfect and have treasures in heaven, he needed to sell all he had and give it to the poor (Matt. 19:21)? Is this our message to the lost (Rom. 10:9-10)?

Every action of Jesus and every teaching He gave, including the parables, need to be examined in context and the question we *should* ask is, "DOES this apply to me under the New Covenant?" In some passages the answer will be yes, and in others, no.

If we don't do this, we will fall into the age-old trap of not recognizing God deals differently with us under grace than He did with those who were under law. Here is a most notable example.

Isaiah 59:1-2
Behold, the Lord's hand is not shortened,
That it cannot save;
Nor His ear heavy,
That it cannot hear.
² But your iniquities have
separated you from your God;
And your sins have hidden His face from you,
So that He will not hear.

We can see two general truths about God in verse 1. He can hear, and He can save. These things are true under any covenant. However, verse two, while true under the Law, is not true under grace. To whom was He speaking? It was to the Israelites who were guilty of the accusations that follow in the rest of the chapter. The law promised a curse for those who did not follow it which involved God not hearing them.

Fellow believers in Jesus, your sins are *forever* forgiven (Heb.10:14). He is *not* holding your sins against you (2 Cor. 5:19, Rom. 4:8). Your sins are continually forgiven (1 Jn. 1:7). He promised to *never* leave you or forsake you for any reason, not ever (Heb. 13:5).

Let us be thankful we are under His New Covenant of grace and faith. When we fail, we need not fear or believe He is hiding His face from us; rather, we may rejoice that He not only forgives us, but is right here with us encouraging us and even working for good the messes we make.

Didn't God love the erring Israelites? Yes, absolutely. Yet He dealt with them as He promised He would. The purpose of the law was to bring the promised Messiah to save the world precisely because He loved the world so much.

Great Things He Has Done

When considering the Proverbs, we think of wisdom, and the Psalms bring us great encouragement and peace. For years the Psalms were a place of refuge when it looked as if my life would crumble into pieces, and the Proverbs instructed me again and again. How blessed we are to have them!

Until my thirties, I meditated upon them, sang them, prayed them, and applied them to my life. Never once in those years did I ever question this practice. When I began to understand the gospel of the grace of God and the difference between the Old and New Covenants (Acts 20:24, Heb. 8:13), I learned I was not under law but grace (Rom. 6:14).

This gradual revelation came softly yet greatly challenged my long-held beliefs—not just beliefs, but the things I'd treasured for so long which had comforted me. While singing a song based on a Psalm, something inside of my spirit would feel uneasy at the words coming out of my mouth. Here is a prime example of a Psalm commonly sung in Christian worship services.

Psalm 51:10-12
Create in me a clean heart, O God,
(He's done that already.)
And renew a steadfast spirit within me.
(He's promised to do this continually.)
[11] Do not cast me away from Your presence,
(He promised to never ever leave us, not ever!)
And do not take Your Holy Spirit from me.
(The Holy Spirit abides in us forever.)
[12] Restore to me the joy of Your salvation.
(He's done that also.)

This is NOT to suggest the Psalms and Proverbs are irrelevant, only that it is important we understand them in context (as we should all Scripture). These were written by those who looked ahead to the coming of Christ. They did not know His indwelling presence and forever forgiveness as we do, nor were the promises yet fulfilled

≈ They could only long for what we already have. ⤜

So, it is perfectly wonderful to read the Psalms and Proverbs and enjoy them as long as we keep their context in mind which includes who wrote them and under what covenant.

However, there is no error to be found in expressing similar sentiments apart from the original text that reflect the New Covenant of grace. We have found many of the Psalms can "work" for us if we simply put them in the present or past tense instead of expressing them as a plea. Here is an example.

> **Psalm 51:10-12** *(New Covenant adaptation)*
> *You have created in me a clean heart, oh God,*
> *And renewed a right spirit in me.*
> *You have promised to never leave me or*
> *forsake me*
> *And Your Spirit abides with me forever.*
> *You have restored to me the joy of my*
> *salvation.*
> *How I praise Your name for what You have*
> *done!*

Hopefully, you can see the difference. In the original Psalm we can hear the heart of the author longing for God, pleading with Him to never leave. When we change it to match our covenant, we can feel the joy and rest of knowing He never will.

The point of demonstrating this truth directly applies to how we read the Psalms and Proverbs as those under the New Covenant. The Jews LOVED the law of God. Unlike us, they were taught by it, led by it, and blessed and cursed by it. It is extremely important we keep this in mind: we are not under the law. The very first Psalm gives us a prime example of the view they had of the law and its importance in their lives.

> **Psalm 1:1-3**
> *Blessed is the man*
> > *Who walks not in the counsel of the*
> > *ungodly,*
> > *Nor stands in the path of sinners,*
> > *Nor sits in the seat of the scornful;*
> ² **But his delight is in the law of the LORD,**
> > **And in His law he meditates day and**
> > **night.**
> ³ *He shall be like a tree*
> > *Planted by the rivers of water,*
> > *That brings forth its fruit in its season,*
> > *Whose leaf also shall not wither;*
> > *And whatever he does shall prosper.*

The above verses were an encouragement to the Jews to make the law of the Lord their priority. In doing so, they could expect strength, fruitfulness, health, and prosperity unlike the ungodly and sinners (those who did not follow the law). It's such a beautiful sentiment though. Why can't we also enjoy it? Consider this New Covenant rendition.

> **Psalm 1:1-3** *(New Covenant adaptation)*
> *Blessed is the man*
> > *Who walks by grace through faith*
> ² *His delight is in* **the grace** *of the LORD,*
> > *And in* **His grace** *he meditates day and*
> > *night.*
> ³ *He shall be like a tree*
> > *Planted by the rivers of water,*
> > *That brings forth its fruit in its season,*
> > *Whose leaf also shall not wither;*
> > *And whatever he does shall prosper.*

This has everything to do with the love of God. If we read the Psalms and Proverbs and inappropriately apply the words to our lives, we will begin to see God's love and blessings as *conditional* on our behavior. We might unnecessarily adopt the emptiness they felt and the veil that separated them from His presence which we now enjoy. However, when we understand the difference between living by grace through faith instead of by law through works, we are set free.

How miserable and confused we can become when we don't understand that law and grace ARE INCOMPATIBLE. When living under law it seems God loves you one day because you prayed and read the Bible and didn't sin, and the next day, His love and blessings for you are diminished because you didn't pray and read the Bible and you sinned (if only an imperfect thought or unkind word). When living under grace, we are truly free from sin and alive unto God.

God is not human, of course, but perhaps you've had a relationship in which it seemed you were loved IF you did what was expected, BUT if you made one mistake, the love was recoiled or at least set aside until you conformed. In fact, in relationships such as that, we never truly feel loved unconditionally, if at all.

My friends, God's love is not like that. He is not holding our sins against us. He is not withdrawing His love if we make a mistake in word or deed. He isn't turning His back on us until we "get right" with Him. He isn't mad at us. He is FOR us, not against us. There is no condemnation, no accusations, no separation, and no damnation for those who are in Him (Rom. 8). He causes all things, yes, even our sins, to work together for our good. This is amazing grace and love in the extreme. [19]

---

[19] "Shall we sin so that grace may abound? God forbid!"

Oh, how I love Your grace!
It is my meditation all the day.[20]

Psalm 119:97 (New Covenant adaptation)

Continuing the Journey

1. Here are some Psalms which are perfect *in context* but need some adjustments when applying similar sentiments to our lives as New Covenant of grace believers. Appreciate how they applied to those under the Old Covenant, and then change the words to reflect our grace/faith/Spirit covenant. You might do this by putting them in the past or present tense or perhaps presenting the New Covenant truth.

   Psalm 6:1
   O LORD, do not rebuke me in Your anger,
   Nor chasten me in Your hot displeasure.
   Psalm 10:1
   Why do You stand afar off, O LORD?
   Why do You hide in times of trouble?
   Psalm 15
   LORD, who may abide in Your tabernacle?
   Who may dwell in Your holy hill?
   ² He who walks uprightly,
   And works righteousness,
   And speaks the truth in his heart;

2. Here are some Psalms and Proverbs which exalt the law. In context, they are perfectly fine because the Jews were under the law. How might these take on a whole new

---

[20] Original Verse: Oh, how I love Your law! It is my meditation all the day.

meaning if we use the terms grace, faith, or Spirit instead of law, works, and flesh?[21]

> **Psalm 19:7-11**
> The **law** of the LORD is perfect, converting the soul;
>> The **testimony** of the LORD is sure,
>> making wise the simple;
> [8] The **statutes** of the LORD are right,
>> rejoicing the heart;
>> The **commandment** of the LORD is pure,
>> enlightening the eyes;
> [9] The **fear** of the LORD is clean, enduring forever;
>> The **judgments** of the LORD are true and righteous altogether.
> [10] More to be desired are they than gold,
>> Yea, than much fine gold;
>> Sweeter also than honey and the honeycomb.
>
> **Proverbs 28:9**
> One who turns away his ear from hearing the law,
> Even his prayer is an abomination.

3. These same truths apply to the words of the Old Testament prophets. We must read them in context. To whom was the prophet speaking? It might not apply to you at all or it may be you can only extract from it an understanding of how God related to them under the law versus how he relates to us now. Consider the following example and/or share other examples that come to mind.

> **Malachi 3:9**
> You are <u>cursed with a curse</u>,
> For you have robbed Me,
> Even this whole nation.

---

[21] "Flesh" can also simply refer to the physical body.

Chapter 7

HE IS WHO HE CLAIMS TO BE

*A*n important component of knowing we are loved by
God is learning about His characteristics. It's important
to note, that unlike many human relationships we experience, God will never disappoint us. Thankfully, God is who
He claims to be, AND He does what He promises to do. Our
understanding and appreciation for the love of God grows as
we learn more about Him.

Many valuable studies are available on the various names
of God in Scripture. These names help us form an understanding of God's character and what He does. El-Shaddai,
for example, reveals God is mightier than any other force that
exists. El-Olam teaches us God's existence is eternal. El-Berith
declares He keeps His covenants, and El-Roi assures us
God sees us.

Other names with which you might be familiar are Yahweh-
Jireh[22] (The Lord Will Provide), Yahweh-Shalom (The Lord is
Peace), Yahweh-Rohi (The Lord is My Shepherd), and Yahweh-
Tsidkenu (The Lord Our Righteousness). These names show
us God will take care of our needs (Phil. 4:9), be at peace with
us (Rom. 8:31), tenderly guide us (Rom. 8:14), and give us His
very righteousness (2 Cor. 5:21)

Then, of course, we have the many beautiful names ascribed
to God the Son, among those being Wonderful Counselor,

---

[22] Feel free to substitute Jehovah for Yahweh, if you prefer.

Mighty God, Prince of Peace, Lamb of God, The Way, The Truth, The Life, The Light of the World, Redeemer, Savior, The Good Shepherd, Overseer of Our Souls, God with Us, High Priest, and Friend. As we remember these names, our minds are enlightened and our hearts are encouraged as we acknowledge His goodness and grace toward us simply by considering who He is.

The names of God show us many things about Him. Now, let us examine some of His names a bit closer in light of what they tell us about His sure love for us.

El-Roi, The God Who Sees

Perhaps one of the most tender aspects describing God is that He sees us. He looks upon us with great affection because we are His special creations. He knows exactly what we feel and what we are thinking. He observes what is going on around us. He sees injustices we face.

He understands when we feel unloved by the human beings in our lives who are supposed to love us. He sees the anguish and heartache this causes us. He sees us when we make mistakes and begin to suffer the consequences of our actions. He doesn't abandon us in our times of need.

He doesn't panic when we worry for He knows the reason. He bids us to cast our cares upon Him because He cares for us. No matter what we experience in this life, we can confidently know He is the God who is looking upon us with love—not to condemn and judge, but to build up and encourage.

> *Seeing then that we have a great High Priest*
> *who has passed through the heavens,*
> *Jesus the Son of God,*
> *let us hold fast our confession*
> *15 For we do not have a High Priest*
> *who cannot sympathize with our weaknesses,*
> *but was in all points tempted as we are,*
> *yet without sin.*
> *16 Let us therefore come boldly to the throne of grace,*
> *that we may obtain mercy*

and find grace to help in time of need.

Hebrews 4:14-16

Yahweh-Jireh

One of the areas afflicting many people is that of provision. Hopefully, we are all working hard to provide for ourselves and our families, even to give to those in need, but sometimes our best efforts are not enough, and we find it difficult to make ends meet or to get out of debt. Beyond the day-to-day necessities, there are situations that arise when we face unexpected losses such as weather-related damage, emergency room and hospital bills, even legal battles we never thought we'd encounter. We can feel so very alone when we experience need.

Thankfully, we are not alone. God is our Provider. He sees our situations, and it is His very nature to help us when we ask. We don't need to deserve His help and we certainly cannot earn it. He supplies what we need to get through any crisis. We need only trust in Him.

"Until now you have asked nothing in My name.
Ask, and you will receive, that your joy may be full."

John 16:24

Yahweh-Rapha

If you have ever felt like a ping pong ball while seeking medical care for yourself or someone you love, bouncing from one physician to another just to figure out what is going on in your body, you will be relieved to know that the God Who Sees actually knows already exactly what is ailing you. The God Who Provides is making sure you will have what you need to get the care you must have. Even better than that, when you start to identify with the woman who spent all her livelihood on physicians, but only grew worse, you will be thankful our God is Yahweh-Rapha, the Lord Our Healer.

Not only is it His nature to heal, He purchased our healing for us at the expense of the wounds of Jesus—pain He endured for all, even His enemies, long before we were born or acknowledged Him. How much more, now that we are His beloved children, will He help us! Believe this and ask!

Who Himself bore our sins in His own body on the tree,
that we, having died to sins,
might live for righteousness—
by whose stripes you were healed.

1 Peter 2:24

Jesus Our Wonderful Counselor

We need a counselor in life, and our counselor is wonderful. Just let this thought touch you. We don't know everything. We don't see everything. Our resources are limited, and without Him, our power sometimes just isn't enough.

Our God loves us. He understands what we experience. He knows what to do next. He will listen without judging. He will correct us if we need instruction. He wants us to share our every concern with Him, and His wisdom is without limit. When no one else on earth can help or understand, He reaches out to take our hands and lovingly guides us.

Likewise the Spirit also helps in our weaknesses.
For we do not know what we should pray for as we ought,
but the Spirit Himself makes intercession for us
with groanings which cannot be uttered.
Now He who searches the hearts
knows what the mind of the Spirit is,
because He makes intercession for the saints
according to the will of God.

Romans 8:26-27

Jesus Our Savior

How blessed we are to have received eternal salvation by the grace of God through faith in Jesus. Yet salvation is not something we experience only once. Jesus is continually our Savior. Perhaps it would help to consider that "to save" means "to rescue." Everyone goes through experiences if life in which they need rescuing. Situations arise in life we don't expect, times for which we are unprepared, and our God is our Savior. When you are falsely accused, He will save you. When your life seems threatened, He will rescue you. If you feel as if you are drowning and sinking for the last time, call on His name— He will help you. Do not be afraid. Only believe.

And Peter answered Him and said,
"Lord, if it is You,
command me to come to You on the water."
29 So He said, "Come."
And when Peter had come down out of the boat
he walked on the water to go to Jesus.
30 But when he saw that the wind was boisterous
he was afraid; and beginning to sink
he cried out, saying, "Lord, save me!"
31 And immediately
Jesus stretched out His hand and caught him.

Matthew 14:28-31

Continuing the Journey

1.   Using some of the other names for God mentioned in the beginning of this chapter or others you recall, explain how they point to God's love for us.

PART 2

No Greater Love

Chapter 8

THE FULNESS OF TIME

---

*A*t a certain point in my adult life, the need to be better acquainted with United States and World History became increasingly evident. So, even with a college degree and two teaching credentials, I determined to take classes at a nearby Community College to fill in the gaps of my global understanding. It was amazing how much there was to learn about my own country's foundations, but it was during my World History class that a picture of how world events came together to prepare for the coming of Christ came into view.[23]

> **Galatians 4:4-5**
> *But when the fullness of the time had come, God sent forth His Son, born of a woman, born under the law, ⁵ to redeem those who were under the law, that we might receive the adoption as sons.*

One doesn't need to be a history scholar to take notice of the grand coming together of events that took place prior to

---

[23] I must give thanks to my instructor at that time, Bruce Clymer, who made the study of history so interesting and who graciously helped me edit this chapter.

Jesus' appearing.[24] As we take a glance at these events, we are able to see the love of God at work throughout history.

As most Christians know, Israel and Judah were taken captive (as God warned them would happen if they did not repent of their rebellion toward Him). Their liberation from this captivity which included the rebuilding of Jerusalem and its wall seem to start a clock ticking toward the coming of Messiah.

Before the Roman Empire came into being, there existed the Roman Republic (509 BC-27 AD). During these years the governing powers were in the hands of senators elected by the people. It was during this time Alexander the Great conquered the Persian Empire. His life and conquests were prophesied by Daniel (Dan. 8:1-8; 18-22). It is thought Alexander was peaceful toward the Jews because a priest showed him from Scripture he was the fulfillment of Daniel's prophecy. Amazingly, all his triumphs took place before he was only 33 years old at which time he died, and his kingdom was divided.

Alexander spread the Greek language and culture wherever he conquered, and Greek became the predominant language of the Mediterranean and Middle East. Greek became so prevalent, that over the centuries the Hebrew Scriptures were gradually translated from Hebrew into Greek. So not only did much of the world speak one language, but the resulting translation we now call the Septuagint made Scripture more accessible for others to read.[25]

Consider how important the Greek language was in the spread of Christianity. Since most of what we refer to as the New Testament was written in Greek, the fact so many were

---

[24] Presented in this chapter is a very condensed summary of events that took place before and after the coming of Christ. Each event is written about extensively elsewhere. It is not my intent to give a detailed account of these things, but rather to show how these happenings set the stage perfectly for the coming of Jesus and the subsequent spread of His gospel.

[25] The translation of the Septuagint itself began in the 3rd century BC and was completed by 132 BC. https://en.wikipedia.org/wiki/Septuagint

literate in Greek facilitated the spread of Christianity both by word and letter. As far as language goes, the timing was perfect for Jesus' physical ministry on earth.

During the years 175-163 BC, a Greek leader named Antiochus IV Epiphanes lead a campaign against the Jews, forcing them to accept the Greek language, culture, and gods. He mandated a death sentence for those who owned or read the Torah (Gen.-Deut.). He plundered the Jewish temple making it a shrine for Zeus and sacrificed a pig on the altar.

This oppression and sacrilege infuriated the Jews causing a godly family of priests named the Maccabees to revolt against him. They led a series of successful wars for independence. This campaign for freedom caused the Jews to more closely guard and follow their faith, nation, language, and culture. They began to reject the foreign gods that had been imposed upon them and endeavored to live holy lives by following the law.

It was during this time the Pharisees and Sadducees came into being. The Sadducees concerned themselves more with political power while the Pharisees were focused on preserving the Jewish faith. Among the Pharisees were the Scribes who were an elite group responsible for copying and preserving the law of God.

Even so, Jerusalem was once again conquered in 63 BC by the Roman General Pompey. He not only killed the priests but dared to enter the Holy of Holies, a place only to be entered by the high priest of Israel. Rather than discourage the Jews, this oppression served to cause them to long for deliverance from the Roman domination. Who better to save them than the promised Messiah? Thus there grew a heightened desire and a "looking" for His appearance.

Rome as an empire began in 27 BC when Gaius Octavius was given the name Augustus by the Roman senate after years of civil war. This is when the Pax Romana began, a time during which there was relative peace and less expansion by military force. This "peace" lasted until 180 AD. Consider the dates. Twenty-seven years before Jesus was born and extending 180 years after, there was a relative peace during which Christianity would be able to make a solid influence that would last until today.

Another factor that greatly contributed to preparing for the "fulness of time" had to do with travel and commerce becoming safer. Roads which were built originally for Roman military expansion were in place for the spreading of the gospel with 50,000 miles extending to all parts of the empire. Many of them were constructed so weather would not be a factor. Some were raised above the ground level or at an angle to make rain run-off possible. Many had drainage canals. Along the roads were milestones which marked the distance to certain destinations. Lodging was available at about one day's journey. Consider how these travelways, which from the Roman perspective, were constructed to aid in military domination, were used by God to make a way for the coming Messiah and for His followers to share the love of God with mankind.

In my mind's eye, I see the love of God in all of this swirling throughout history causing even the evil intent of governments in the world, to work together to bring about the perfect setting to fulfill His promises and pour out His love. When that moment came, He sent His Son to save the world and demonstrated His love by dying for us.

But when the kindness and the love
of God our Savior toward man appeared,
[5] not by works of righteousness which we have done,
but according to His mercy He saved us.

Titus 3:4-5

Continuing the Journey

1. Perhaps while reading through this lesson, you thought of other historical events that contributed to preparing for the coming of the promised Messiah. Feel free to share or make note of them.

2. Most of us have multiple happenings going on in our lives at one time. Some of them are pleasant; others are tumultuous. God is not sending evil into our lives in any way. Evil causes evil. Consider, though, God is involved in our lives, too, causing all things to work together for our good—including the efforts of those who oppose us to destroy us and even our own mistakes. Can you look back and see how God worked all things together for your good in certain situations?

3. Can you look ahead in faith and believe He is good and He will continue to work your current circumstances together for your good?

Chapter 9

THE APPEARANCE OF HIS LOVE

John 3:16-21

*"For God so **loved** the world that He **gave** His only begotten Son, that whoever believes in Him should not perish but have everlasting life. [17] "For God did not send His Son into the world to condemn the world, but that the world through Him might be saved. [18] He who believes in Him is not condemned; but he who does not believe is condemned already, because he has not believed in the name of the only begotten Son of God. [19] And this is the condemnation, that the light has come into the world, and men loved darkness rather than light, because their deeds were evil." [20] For everyone practicing evil hates the light and does not come to the light, lest his deeds should be exposed. [21] But he who does the truth comes to the light, that his deeds may be clearly seen, that they have been done in God."*

The fulness of time came to a world full of darkness, depravity, and desperation. The Jewish nation, at least, had faith in God and hope the Messiah would come and save them, but the Gentiles had no hope and were without God in the world (Eph. 2:12).

O, holy night
The stars are brightly shining.
It is the night of our dear Savior's birth.
Long lay the world
In sin and error pining
Till He appeared, and the soul felt its worth.
A thrill of hope the weary world rejoices
For yonder breaks
A new and glorious morn.[26]

His miraculous conception, His humble birth, His baptism by John, His earthly ministry, His redeeming death, and His welcomed resurrection, opened the heavens to pour out His light and love for all who would believe.

What condescension
Bringing us redemption
That in the dead of night
Not one faint hope in sight
God gracious tender
Laid aside His splendor
Stooping to woo to win
To save my soul.

O, how I love Him
How I adore Him
My breath my sunshine
My all in all.
The great Creator
Became my Savior
And all God's fullness
Dwelleth in Him[27]

---

[26] "O, Holy Night," music composed by Adolphe Adam in 1847, words by Placide Cappeau, Public Domain
[27] William E. Booth-Clibborn, Public Domain

Most of us can look back to a time in our lives when most of our attention was focused on ourselves. Some of us indulged our every whim, living with the primary goal of pleasing ourselves in the most egotistical of ways. Others set high goals and standards for success in life, but still with the intent of pleasing themselves. A rare few chose to sacrifice for the sake of others, but sometimes this also was for self-satisfaction or to find meaning in life. Whether living the most debase of lifestyles or appearing to everyone else to have it together, the self-centered life does not satisfy. Thankfully, God's love stepped in the scene of our individual lives, too.

> **Titus 3:3-7**
> *For we ourselves were also once foolish, disobedient, deceived, serving various lusts and pleasures, living in malice and envy, hateful and hating one another.* **⁴ But when the kindness and the love of God our Savior toward man appeared,** *⁵ not by works of righteousness which we have done, but according to His mercy He saved us, through the washing of regeneration and renewing of the Holy Spirit, ⁶ whom He poured out on us abundantly through Jesus Christ our Savior, ⁷ that having been justified by His grace we should become heirs according to the hope of eternal life.*

Many of us can remember when the kindness and the love of God appeared to us. He washed us of all our sins, renewed us by His Spirit and justified us by His grace. Here is some very good news. Not only did God save us in the past, but He will rescue us today.

Your life may be chaos right now, and you may be hurting in ways that are either your own doing through wrong choices or very possibly you are in pain because someone you love is making your life miserable. No matter who or what is to blame for what you are experiencing, God's love is ready to appear toward you again.

His rescue won't be because you are perfect, and it won't be withheld from you because you are at fault. If you reach out to Him this very moment, His mercy and love will reach out to save you. He will renew you, and He will do so abundantly. He will do this because He really does love you, not just initially when you accepted Him, but throughout your life.

Reach out to him right now—empty handed—with no excuses or justification, except by His grace. Your soul will once again feel its worth as His love and grace appear.

For the Scripture says, "Whoever believes in Him [whoever adheres to, trusts in, and relies on Him] will not be disappointed [in his expectations]." [12] *For there is no distinction between Jew and Gentile; for the same Lord is Lord over all [of us], and [He is] abounding in riches (blessings) for all who call on Him [in faith and prayer].* [13] *For "whoever calls on the name of the Lord [in prayer] will be saved."*

Romans 10:11-13 AMP

Continuing the Journey

1. What thoughts come to mind when considering the love God demonstrated when He sent His Son to earth to redeem mankind?

2. Bring to remembrance how God rescued you in the past. How can remembering these miraculous events encourage us in our current situations?

Chapter 10

IF YOU'VE SEEN ME

---

*D*o you ever imagine Jesus is sitting near you? Or do you wish that for just one hour you could talk to Him in person—sharing each one of your concerns and asking Him those questions you've always pondered? Sometimes when I'm troubled, I picture Him in the room with me. Reaching out my hand toward Him for comfort, I imagine He tenderly takes it removing all my concerns.

If He *were* to appear to me, I'm sure I would first faint! Then I would start crying and thank Him for His love for me, and for the tender way He's led me all of my life. I wouldn't think to ask questions, but just by sitting in His presence, I would already know the answers.

What would He say? Perhaps it would be, "Cathy, I'm proud of you. You believe in me in the good times and bad, and this brings pleasure to my heart. I want you to know and believe I love you always. I'm with you as you write this book. I want my people to know I love them, and I will use you to share this truth. Don't allow your insecurities to hold you back from declaring these glad tidings—that I love my children more intensely than they will ever know. Be strong and persevere. You can do this! I called you to preach the gospel to the saved, and you will. I will be with you."

As I wrote the above words, I became aware that God was saying just that to my heart, and my eyes filled with tears, as once again the realization that He is with us always, ready to speak to us was made clear. We don't need to see Him to hear from Him.

All Christians long to be in the physical presence of our Savior, but the very fact we do not see Him results in a special blessing for us. We find this truth in a conversation between Jesus and Thomas. Jesus had risen from the dead. Many had seen Him, but Thomas missed out. He said to the other disciples he would not believe unless He could put his hands into Jesus' wounds (thus the expression "doubting Thomas"). When Jesus appeared to Thomas, He invited him to do what he'd asked, but Thomas instead proclaimed, "My Lord and My God!" Jesus answered him and said,

> *"Thomas, because you have seen Me, you have believed.*
> *Blessed are those who have not seen*
> *and yet have believed."*

Jesus was speaking of those who would follow, of us— those who believe in Him even though we have never seen Him. Therefore, we are blessed. Think about that. Millions of people throughout the centuries have believed in the resurrection of Jesus Christ without the benefit of having seen Him, and God the Father personally rejoices over each one who has believed in His Son.

1 Peter 1:6-8
*In this you greatly rejoice, though now for a little while, if need be, you have been grieved by various trials, ⁷ that the genuineness of your faith, being much more precious than gold that perishes, though it is tested by fire, may be found to praise, honor, and glory at the revelation of Jesus Christ, ⁸ **whom having not seen you love. Though now you do not see Him, yet believing, you rejoice with joy inexpressible and full of glory.***

You Shall All Know Me

When we were young adults back in the 1970's, there was a strong emphasis on "knowing God" and "knowing God *more.*" We had no problem adopting this goal because if there was "more" of God for us, we wanted all that was available. It sounded a noble endeavor, but it was not a needed one. This is because one of the principle provisions of the New Covenant is that we all know Him.

> ### Jeremiah 31:34
> "No more shall every man teach his neighbor, and every man his brother, saying, 'Know the Lord,' **for they all shall know Me**, from the least of them to the greatest of them, says the Lord. For I will forgive their iniquity, and their sin I will remember no more."

The Hebrew word for "more" in the above verse is "ode, ode" and means "again, repeatedly, still, more: - again, all life long, at all, henceforth, (any) longer, (any) more."[28] Under the New Covenant, His promise is we will not (and thus, need not) repeatedly (all our lives long) teach each other to know the Lord. Think about the peace this can bring! We already know Him. He made this possible when He forgave us and promised to remember our sins no more. There is nothing preventing us from knowing Him.[29]

---

[28] Strong's Hebrew and Greek Dictionaries

[29] The author is aware that two different Greek words in this passage are used. The first is **ginosko** which is often used as being acquainted with something or someone. The other Greek word is **eido**. This word implies a more careful knowledge and observation. Some very excellent scholars say the first "know" refers the kind of knowing man had of God before the cross under the law, and the second word is the kind of "knowing" we have under the New Covenant. I cannot deny this possibility, though Paul used the word **ginosko** when he said he gave up everything to "know" the Lord. Others noted the words are sometimes used interchangeably. Additionally, Spanish

Perhaps it comes to your mind that Paul said he wanted to "know Him" as proof we too need to know Him. Since this is a common teaching, it's worth taking a moment to examine what Paul was saying in context. May the Lord reveal this to your heart even before I explain it.

> **Philippians 3:7-10**
> *But what things were gain to me, these I have counted loss for Christ. ⁸ Yet indeed I also count all things loss for the excellence of the knowledge of Christ Jesus my Lord, for whom I have suffered the loss of all things, and count them as rubbish, that I may gain Christ ⁹ and be found in Him, not having my own righteousness, which is from the law, but that which is through faith in Christ, the righteousness which is from God by faith; ¹⁰ **that I may know Him** and the power of His resurrection—*

When did Paul become righteous by faith? When did he gain Christ? When did he give up all things? When was He found in Him? **When he believed.** He formerly put his confidence in his own righteousness (from the law), but he forsook this self-righteousness and received the righteousness that can only be attained by faith in Christ.

**When we put our faith in Christ,
when we receive His righteousness,
we gain Christ, and we are found in Him—
⁂ AND we know Him. ⁂**

---

has two different words for "know" with similar connotations as the Greek definitions (conocer and saber). The Reina Valera translation of Hebrews 8:11 chose to translate **ginosko and eido** both as "conocer". Since I didn't think this was crucial to my point that we all know Him under the New Covenant, I only elaborated here.

When you came to God through Jesus, you likely instantly were aware you had a relationship with Him. He didn't seem like a stranger to you. You talked to Him. He talked to you. He began teaching you even before you opened a Bible, and when you did open your Bible, He opened the meaning to your heart. You might have proclaimed joyfully that Christianity isn't a religion; it's a relationship with Jesus Christ. You basked in this joy of knowing God for days, months, perhaps even years.

Then someone came along and told you that you could and should know God more. Maybe you thought, "If there is more, I want it," and then asked how to get it. Someone you trusted, gave you a list of how to know God or how to know Him more. Then as a sheep led to the slaughter, you happily began to try to fulfill the list. You didn't think to challenge anything you were told.

At first one might have benefitted from the satisfaction that comes from being disciplined, especially if one's former lifestyle was very disorganized. There is a certain sense of accomplishment that comes from checking off a list as we complete it. Others though, who never were able to fulfill these perceived requirements to know God better, began to experience feelings of considerable failure before God. Gradually, the joy of knowing God dimmed as the list continued to grow and many became estranged from Christ even though their goal was to get closer to Him and know Him more (Gal.5:4).

Here's the good news. We already know God. We don't need to endlessly teach each other to know God. We don't need to *do* anything to know Him. Get rid of those lists that supposedly bring us "closer" to God. We are perfectly close to Him, not because of our discipline in prayer, but because of His blood which brought us close to Him in the first place, and we do know Him because He has forgiven our sins and remembers them no more. Glory to God forevermore!

Getting to Know All about Him

There is a distinction that must be made between knowing God and learning more about Him. This happens through study of the Scripture and experience walking with Him. Each time we study who He is and each time we experience His power in our lives and witness His faithfulness, we learn more *about* Him.

When we got married, of course David and I knew each other—enough to entrust our lives to each other. We had a relationship. Yet there were things *about* each other to be learned as we shared our opinions and observed each other as we went through life together. Through happy days and times of mourning, we learned new intricacies about each other. As we parented our children, we observed new aspects of each other's personalities. We watched each other grow, too, from nineteen-year-old buddies into the almost 64-year-old friends we are today.

The Bible is full of stories and descriptions and examples that help us clearly define attributes of God's loving character. We learn about Him, not because we do *not* know Him; **but because we do**.

There can be no greater example of this than observing the life of Christ as recorded in Matthew, Mark, Luke, and John. Through these firsthand accounts of what Jesus did and said, we are able to get to know more about Him and His great love for us.

> *1 John 1:1-4 (Author of the Gospel of John)*
> *That which was from the beginning, which we have heard, which we have seen with our eyes, which we have looked upon, and our hands have handled, concerning the Word of life— 2 the life was manifested, and we have seen, and bear witness, and declare to you that eternal life which was with the Father and was manifested to us— 3 that which we have seen and heard we declare to you, that you also may have fellowship with us; and truly our fellowship is with the Father and with His Son Jesus Christ. 4 And these things we write to you that your joy may be full.*

Seeing the life of Jesus reveals to us the heart of God because Jesus is God, and His actions are one with the Father's. Consider this powerful declaration made by Paul in Colossians 1:15 (AMP).

**He is the exact living image
[the essential manifestation] of the unseen God
[the visible representation of the invisible].**

To know more about the God we cannot see, we have the life of Jesus which is recorded for us to bring to life who He is. Since He is the visible image of the invisible God, His every word and deed give us information about God the Father.

We can also gather information that negates any adverse image we may have developed of God by carefully observing what He did *not* do and did *not* say.

If you want to know more about God and understand what God's love for you looks like, observe the life of Christ. What you see in Him, is true about the Father. You can see God is love in every word He spoke, each act of kindness He displayed, every miracle He performed, and by the death He died for us. This immense act of love continues to speak to us throughout our journey of rediscovering His love for us.

*Jesus said,
"He who has seen Me
has seen the Father."*

John 14:9

Continuing the Journey

Several years ago, I attended a conference. At one point, the speaker asked us to take a moment and imagine Jesus was right in front of us. Then we were to think of what He would say. I remember the very clear implication of her message was He would tell us what was *wrong* with us and insist we get our acts together, so I braced myself for such as I went along with the exercise.

To my delighted surprise, what it seemed Jesus said to me was, "I love you." I smiled and began to cry.

1. If you'd like, take a few minutes to remind yourself Jesus is always with you. Imagine you could see Him in this moment. What do you think He would He say to you personally?

2. As you continue reading this book, stop now and then to talk to Him remembering He is with you always.

Chapter 11

NO GREATER LOVE

It didn't "just happen"
A man on a cross
Who though He had all
Considered it loss.
He humbled Himself
And a servant became.
It didn't "just happen"
Nor shall it again.

People are searching
For someone to care
Someone who'll promise
To always be there.
Their eyes have been blinded
They don't want to see
That someone is Jesus
And always will be.[30]

*O*nly a few years ago, it came to me that the practice of communion should not only be a remembrance of the suffering and death Jesus endured but also a reminder of His love for us.

---

[30] "It Didn't Just Happen", second half of a song by C. D. Hildebrand, 1982

John 15:13
Greater love has no one than this, than to lay down one's life for his friends.

Jesus laid down His life for us. Why? Because He loves us. Yes, He was providing for our salvation and forgiveness, but why? Because He loves us. Why did He suffer? He loves us. Why did He endure false accusations and insults? Why did He submit Himself to the humiliating unjust death on the cross? Because He loves us. He loves us!

Ephesians 2:4-5 AMP
But God, who is rich in mercy, because of His great love with which He loved us, [5] even when we were dead in trespasses, made us alive together with Christ (by grace you have been saved).

The proof of His love remains forever because His love continues forever. Yes, He showed us He loved us by dying for us, but that demonstration is God's *ongoing* way of proving His love for us.

Romans 5:8-9
But God demonstrates His own love toward us, in that while we were still sinners, Christ died for us. [9] Much more then, having now been justified by His blood, we shall be saved from wrath through Him.

Prior to this passage, Paul writes that it would be very rare for someone to die for a righteous person, and that someone might be willing to die for a good person. This is an expression of human love apart from God. This is immediately followed by, "But God," which sets up the rest of this glorious message. Paul is *contrasting* human love with divine love. Human love has limitations and qualifications quite unlikely to be extended toward an enemy. But God's love reached out to us through the cross while we were still sinners and His adversaries to reconcile us to Himself with His own love—not only to save us from sin and wrath through His death, but to continue saving us through His resurrection and life.

The use of "demonstrates" as the interpretation of the Greek word **sunistēmi** in my preferred translation of the Bible, the NKJV, does not fully communicate to us the full meaning. It merits our time to elaborate.

The KJV uses the word "commendeth," which adds a much different dimension than "demonstrates."

> *In Ellicott's Commentary for English Readers we read, "The English word (commendeth) happily covers the **double** meaning of the Greek. The same word is used (1) of things in the sense of 'prove' or 'establish,' here and in Romans 3:5; (2) of persons in the sense of 'recommend,' in Romans 16:1."*

So, God proves and establishes the fact of His love for us and recommends His love to us via the fact Christ died for us.

> *Wuest comments, "'Commends' is **sunistēmi**, 'to put together by combining or comparing, hence to show, prove, establish, exhibit.' The word means here ... 'to hold up to favorable view, to recommend.' Denney says, 'How greatly is this utmost love of man surpassed by the love of God. He commends, or rather makes good, presents in its true and unmistakable character... His own love toward us.'"*

Often, when trying to ascertain the significance of a word in the Bible, I will look in the older Spanish translations (since I speak Spanish). It delighted me to find the word "encarecer" for **sunistēmi** in the RVA.[31] "Encarecer" in Spanish means both to raise the value and to praise the worth of something.

❧ God presents His highly valued love to us as being worthy of our praise. ❧

Perhaps just as significant in our understanding of this passage is that **sunistēmi** is used in the present tense. God is right now proving/showing/recommending favorably His own love for us by the fact He gave His Son in death for us. His love is already on display and speaks to us today.

If you want to be assured of God's love for you, look at Jesus on the cross. Remember that while dying there "God was in Christ, reconciling the world to Himself, not holding their trespasses against them," (2 Cor. 5:19).

> **Romans 5:18-19**
> *Therefore, as through one man's offense*
> *judgment came to all men*
> *resulting in condemnation*
> *even so through one Man's righteous act*
> *the free gift came to all men,*
> *resulting in justification of life.*
> *[19]For as by one man's disobedience*
> *many were made sinners,*
> *so also by one Man's obedience*
> *many will be made righteous.*

Jesus said, "For God so loved the world, that He gave His only begotten Son." Many interpret the word "so" in terms of "so much," and yes, He does love us *so* much. However, the word "so" means "in this manner." In what manner did God

---

[31] "The Reina-Valera Antigua was first translated and published in 1569 by Casiodoro de Reina, after twelve years of intensive work, and later put out in 1602 in revised form by Cipriano de Valera, who gave more than twenty years of his life to its revision and improvement."- biblegateway.com

show us He loves us—by giving His Son in death so we will not perish but have everlasting life.

By this the love of God is revealed to us
that God has sent His one and only Son into the world
so that we might live through Him.

1 John 4:9 MOUNCE

Continuing the Journey

1. In future chapters, we will discuss the many reasons Christians feel isolated from His love, but maybe you already know some affecting you. Record here where you are right now in your understanding of God's love for you and what you currently think might be keeping you from fully knowing and believing the love God has for you.

2. How does knowing the death of Jesus is God's way of recommending His own love to us (as something to be praised) affect you personally?

Chapter 12

NOTHING CAN SEPARATE US

*P*erhaps you also gradually adopted the belief that God's presence is something we need to "enter," that it comes and goes based on our righteousness or intensity of worship, or that our closeness with God is based on our diligence in prayer and our level of personal holiness.

For us, "seeking God" required we pray daily (for 60 minutes—not one minute less), read the Bible daily, attend all church services regularly, give ten percent plus more, get involved in multiple ministries, do what Jesus would do, be holy in every thought, word, and deed, and do so purposefully and with much fervor. This list grew regularly as each new teaching trend hit the sermon circuit.

If we fell short in any area, this would explain to us why it felt as if God was distancing Himself from us. For me, it seemed He was motionless with His arms folded waiting for me to "get it together" spiritually. David's thoughts were more intense to the extent of believing God was not only disappointed in the lack of his spiritual and ministerial accomplishments, but also *ashamed* of him—a sure ticket to depression. You see, there was nothing we wanted more in life than to please God, and we never felt we did.

Oh, yes, we knew this passage.

Romans 8:35, 38-39
Who shall separate us from the love of Christ?

> *Shall tribulation, or distress, or persecution, or famine, or nakedness, or peril, or sword? [38] For I am persuaded that neither death nor life, nor angels nor principalities nor powers, nor things present nor things to come, [39] nor height nor depth, nor any other created thing, shall be able to separate us from the love of God which is in Christ Jesus our Lord.*

What a glorious truth to know nothing can separate us from God's love, and yet grace can be nullified with ifs, ands, and buts—conditions, additions, and exceptions to God's glorious provisions (Gal. 2:21). This is what happened in our lives as we were exposed to erroneous teachings such as this one which was delivered with great intensity.

> *"You will notice in Romans 8:35-39 this does NOT include **you**!!! It does NOT include **your** SIN. You CAN separate **yourself** from God. Your sin DOES separate you. God hates sin. He cannot look upon sin. He cannot look upon you when you sin. Not until you stop your sinning and seek forgiveness can your relationship with Him be restored."*

We swallowed this lie—hook, line, and sinker for way too many painful years until, thankfully, we began to understand "our sins and lawless deeds he remembers no more," and that "nothing" means nothing and that included us, even if we sinned.

Who can separate us? No one—not even we ourselves. What can separate us? Nothing—not even our sins. Nothing can separate us from the love God has for us. Say it out loud and with conviction,

**"Nothing can separate me
from my God or His love for me.
Nothing and no one!"**

Let me also affirm something which is crucial to us understanding that nothing can put distance between us and God: We don't *need* to "enter" His presence. We don't *need* to be taken into the Holy of Holies, my brothers and sisters. **We are already there** (Heb. 10:19-22, 6:19). When the veil was torn by the hand of God as Jesus died, He made a way for us to enter in and there we *remain*. Not only are we in the Holy of Holies, the Holy Spirit resides within each one of us forever (Jn. 14:15-17). More than that, we are one spirit with Him.

> ### *1 Corinthians 6:17*
> *But he who is joined to the Lord is one spirit with Him.*

You cannot get closer to God than having His holy presence living within you. You cannot improve on being one spirit with Jesus. When you pray, you need not look to the heavens because He is already right here. This blessed gift cannot be taken away from you ever.

He [God] Himself has said, I will not in any way fail you nor give you up nor leave you without support. [I will] not, [I will] not, [I will] not in any degree leave you helpless nor forsake nor let [you] down (relax My hold on you)! [Assuredly not!]

Hebrews 13:5 AMP

Continuing the Journey

1. Take another look at Romans 8:35-39. How does the list of forces against us seek to make us feel separated from God's love?

2. Define the word "nothing." Does that include everything?

3. Share how the truth we cannot be separated from God's love makes us overcomers?

4. Take a few minutes to consider 1 Corinthians 6:17 (above). How significant is this truth when considering our permanent closeness to God?

Chapter 13

SEEKING GOD'S LOVE

*T*here are many Christians today who would admit they don't "feel" His love. Since you are reading this book, perhaps you are one of them or you know someone who struggles in this area. Having been through such a time as this personally, I can testify there is nothing more *miserable* for a Christian than not having confidence in God's love.

We pray with longing hearts and tears, but there seems to be a divine silence. We think perhaps we are "going through a dry spell or a valley" or God has "put us on the shelf" or we are being "tested" to prove we will serve God no matter how we feel. If this describes your sentiments, you are not alone.

To alleviate this pain, many begin to sing their woes of desperation, hunger, and thirst and cry their hearts out at the church altar which might produce some momentary respite, but no lasting relief. Some will double down on their "spiritual disciplines" or seek out new ones to practice, determined to draw "closer" to God so they can experience His love. The solution for others is to go on extreme mission trips or become more involved in local ministry sometimes to the point of neglecting their own families. There are those as well, who will do extended fasts or take vows of poverty or of permanent celibacy if only to once again sense His love and favor. Still others attend seminars or read books to try and figure out what is "wrong"—to go deeper—to fix it.

Countless more seek out to "experience" God's love by attending churches or conferences with a reputation as being places one can *feel* the love of God. For a few hours or days, maybe even weeks, they are emotionally charged, but just as some children experience a let-down after the highs of church camp, they are dry again, and will travel hundreds, even thousands of miles, to once again sense His presence and love.

These endless efforts illustrate how crucial it is for us to know we are loved by our God.

How empty we feel living in uncertainty. Some blame God. Others blame themselves, but only a few figure out something is wrong. It is *not, not, not* ok to feel unloved by God. This is not to say you should feel guilty about it, but rather, **God doesn't want you to *ever* feel unloved by Him**, and we should *not, not, not* accept it as "normal."

When we sense something isn't quite right, it is best to confront the issue, no matter what. If you've been wondering why you feel miserable, God wants you to figure it out, and this is one reason I'm writing this book—to help you find your way back to your first love—the joy of knowing and believing God loves you immensely and without condition.

Parts 3 and 4 of this book will discuss some of the experiences and teachings that can block a clear vision of God's love for us, but before we begin the consideration of those things, let us first confront some common misconceptions in the church today which contribute to the false idea that we need to find Him or His love.

Misconception #1 Looking for God

Have you heard this verse? "You will seek Me and find Me, when you search for Me with all your heart," (Jer. 29:13). "Feeling empty? Does God seem far away?" we are asked. "Then seek God with all of your heart and you will find Him," we are told.

The biggest problem with this statement, is the idea you *need* to find God as a born-again Christian. You do not. That happened when you believed in Him, and He has never left you or forsaken you. His Spirit is living inside of you permanently.

◈ We don't need to find something we already have. ◈

Then what does this verse mean? Like any other passage, it must be taken in context.

> ### Jeremiah 29:10-14
> *For thus says the Lord: After seventy years are completed at Babylon, I will visit you and perform My good word toward you and cause you to return to this place. ¹¹ For I know the thoughts that I think toward you, says the Lord, thoughts of peace and not of evil, to give you a future and a hope. ¹² Then you will call upon Me and go and pray to Me, and I will listen to you. ¹³ And you will seek Me and find Me, when you search for Me with all your heart. ¹⁴ I will be found by you, says the Lord, and I will bring you back from your captivity; I will gather you from all the nations and from all the places where I have driven you, says the Lord, and I will bring you to the place from which I cause you to be carried away captive.*

Those words were spoken to, "the people whom Nebuchadnezzar had carried away captive from Jerusalem to Babylon," (vs.1). As explained in Chapter 3, different covenants include different ways in which believers relate to God. His indwelling presence was not enjoyed by Israel at that time, and they were in exile. We do not need to seek God in the sense of finding Him. This has already taken place.

Misconception #2 Seeking God's Kingdom

This following verse is also used inappropriately. "Seek first the kingdom of God and His righteousness, and all these things will be added to you." To whom was Jesus teaching this principle? The Jews. We Christians already sought God's kingdom, and indeed found it and were brought into it by grace through faith.

> **Colossians 1:13**
> *He has delivered us from the power of darkness and conveyed us into the kingdom of the Son of His love.*
> **James 2:5**
> *Listen, my beloved brethren: Has God not chosen the poor of this world to be rich in faith and heirs of the kingdom which He promised to those who love Him?*

This same principle holds true for this verse: "Blessed are those who hunger and thirst for righteousness, for they shall be filled." We sought after righteousness. We found it by grace through faith. He made us the very righteousness of God (2 Cor. 5:21). Now that we are filled we need only give thanks for this glorious gift.

Misconception #3 Hungering and Thirsting for God

Most of us have been told something is wrong with us if we do not have a hunger and thirst for God in our hearts. This is not true, my friend. In fact, there is a *reason* we don't have a hunger and thirst for God. The reason for this is so obvious; how could we have missed it for so many years?

> **John 6:35**
> *And Jesus said to them, "I am the bread of life. He who comes to Me shall **never hunger**, and he who believes in Me shall **never thirst**."*

Jesus did not come to earth, suffer, die, and rise from the dead so we would feel hungry or thirsty for Him, and it is fair for us to examine why we feel this way. He came to give us life. We need to *cultivate* hunger and thirst only because we aren't *supposed* to be hungering or thirsting for God—ever again. Yes, we go through difficult times that can be devastating, but when it comes to our relationship with God, we have a super-abundance of all we need.

Misconception #4 Desperation

Let us define "desperate." Webster's first definition is as follows:

> *a : having lost hope*
> *b : giving no ground for hope*

Really? If there is anything a Christian has, it is hope, for we serve the God of hope.

Romans 15:13
Now may the God of hope fill you with all joy
and peace in believing, that you may abound
in hope by the power of the Holy Spirit.

When we are convinced of God's love for us, it is more natural to hope in God than to fret. We may *feel* desperate; things might *look* desperate, but we are not ever without hope. No matter what happens in this life, we can hope in the God of hope who fills us with all joy and peace in believing in Him and in His love. Instead of striving to stay "desperate for God," let us endeavor to abound in hope by the power of the Holy Spirit. Let us not continually exalt our woes and troubles; rather, let us exalt our God for whom nothing is impossible.

> *Now **hope** does not disappoint,*
> *because the **love of God***
> *has been poured out in our hearts*
> *by the Holy Spirit who was given to us.*

Romans 5:5

Continuing the Journey

1. Sometimes we allow traditions to override truth. Jesus promised we would never hunger or thirst again, but we insist on hungering and thirsting for God. We have every reason to hope in God, and yet we set up a false noble pursuit of being desperate for God. Share how the truths in this chapter can set us free to once again be not only satisfied but overflowing with everlasting life.

2. When we pray, we often think of God as "up there somewhere" instead of in us. How does this false perception feed into the idea of being hungry, thirsty, and desperate for Him?

3. How do the misconceptions presented in this chapter give us the impression God is far way?

Chapter 14

BLESSED

We know desperate people do desperate things, and it is very sad there are thousands of Christians in the body of Christ today who are so desperate to hear from God, experience His presence, see His power, and feel His love that they will abandon the truth in the written word of God and turn to other mediators whose names are not "Jesus."

Please hear me. You do not need to seek extra-Biblical experiences to know God's love.[32] You already experienced the most amazing evidence of His love that ever existed on earth!

> *1 John 3:1*
> *Behold what manner of love the Father has bestowed on us, that we should be called children of God!*

By grace through faith in Jesus, you became a child of God—a new creation created by God Himself.

> *1 Corinthians 5:17*
> *Therefore, if anyone is in Christ, he is a new creation; old things have passed away; behold, all things have become new.*

---

[32] An extra-Biblical experience is one which is not presented in the New Testament.

You were redeemed with His blood being forgiven of all sin forever.

Ephesians 1:7
In Him we have redemption through His blood, the forgiveness of sins, according to the riches of His grace

You were set free from the power of sin and death.

Romans 8:2
For the law of the Spirit of life in Christ Jesus has made me free from the law of sin and death.

You received everlasting life.

1 John 5:13
These things I have written to you who believe in the name of the Son of God, that you may know that you have eternal life, and that you may continue to believe in the name of the Son of God.

His Holy Spirit abides in you forever.

John 14:16-17
"And I will pray the Father, and He will give you another Helper, that He may abide with you forever— [17] the Spirit of truth, whom the world cannot receive, because it neither sees Him nor knows Him; but you know Him, for He dwells with you and will be in you."

You daily walk in His Spirit.

Romans 8:14
For as many as are led by the Spirit of God,

these are sons of God.

The power that raised Jesus Christ from the dead lives in you continually.

Romans 8:11
But if the Spirit of Him who raised Jesus from the dead dwells in you, He who raised Christ from the dead will also give life to your mortal bodies through His Spirit who dwells in you.

Every spiritual blessing there is, you already possess. You have been adopted by the living God. You are accepted in Him.

Ephesians 1:3-6
Blessed be the God and Father of our Lord Jesus Christ, who has blessed us with every spiritual blessing in the heavenly places in Christ, ⁴ just as He chose us in Him before the foundation of the world, that we should be holy and without blame before Him in love, ⁵ having predestined us to adoption as sons by Jesus Christ to Himself, according to the good pleasure of His will, ⁶ to the praise of the glory of His grace, by which He made us accepted in the Beloved.

All things that pertain to life and godliness are already yours.

2 Peter 1:2-4
Grace and peace be multiplied to you in the knowledge of God and of Jesus our Lord, ³ as His divine power has given to us all things that pertain to life and godliness, through the knowledge of Him who called us by glory and virtue, ⁴ by which have been given to us exceedingly great and precious promises, that through these you may be partakers of the

> *divine nature, having escaped the corruption
> that is in the world through lust.*

Healing and miracles are already yours.

> **1 Peter 2:24**
> *Who Himself bore our sins in His own body on
> the tree, that we, having died to sins, might live
> for righteousness—by whose stripes you were
> healed.*

We don't need anyone to help us hear from God. Jesus Christ died to give us direct access. God is OUR God and we know Him. Amazingly, we have the mind of Christ.

> **1 Corinthians 2:9-12, 16**
> *But as it is written:*
> *"Eye has not seen, nor ear heard,*
> *Nor have entered into the heart of man*
> *The things which God has prepared for those
> who love Him."*
> *¹⁰ But God has revealed them to us through
> His Spirit. For the Spirit searches all things,
> yes, the deep things of God. ¹¹ For what man
> knows the things of a man except the spirit
> of the man which is in him? Even so no one
> knows the things of God except the Spirit of
> God. ¹² Now we have received, not the spirit of
> the world, but the Spirit who is from God, that
> we might know the things that have been freely
> given to us by God.*
> *¹⁶ For "who has known the mind of the Lord
> that he may instruct Him?"* **But we have the
> mind of Christ.**

You have been given an anointing. You do not need to depend on anyone or anything else to hear from God.

1 John 2:27
But the anointing which you have received from Him abides in you, and you do not need that anyone teach you; but as the same anointing teaches you concerning all things, and is true, and is not a lie, and just as it has taught you, you will abide in Him.

You have the wisdom of God.

1 Corinthians 1:30
But of Him you are in Christ Jesus, who became for us wisdom from God—and righteousness and sanctification and redemption—

You are the righteousness of God in Christ Jesus.

2 Corinthians 5:21 *MOUNCE*
He made Him who knew no sin to be a sin-offering for us, so that in Him we might become the righteousness of God.

You are already in His presence and His presence is in you. You don't need a formula to talk to Him. He tore the veil that separated you. You are His sheep and you hear His voice.

Ephesians 2:4-6
But God, who is rich in mercy, because of His great love with which He loved us, ⁵ even when we were dead in trespasses, made us alive together with Christ (by grace you have been saved), ⁶ and raised us up together, and made us sit together in the heavenly places in Christ Jesus.

Mark 15:38
Then the veil of the temple (that separated us from the holiest place of His presence) was

torn in two from top to bottom.
John 10:27
*My sheep hear My voice, and I know them,
and they follow Me.*

You are already as close to God as anyone can be.

1 Corinthians 6:17
*But he who is joined to the Lord is one spirit
with Him.*

What did you do to receive all of this? Believe in Jesus. That is all. How do you walk in all of this? Believe in Jesus. That's it! The miracle worker is God. We simply receive all He has provided for us.

◈ **Nothing you do will make better what you already have in Jesus.** ◈

We will never be completely content with what He has given until we rid ourselves of those things which nullify the grace and love of God for us. We must be aware there are teachings and practices in the body of Christ which are false, and sincerely ask God to open our eyes to see them.

*Oh, the depth of the riches
both of the wisdom and knowledge of God!*

Romans 11:33

Continuing the Journey

1. Look over this chapter again and consider the blessings God has given us. How do these things enable us to live by grace through faith?

2. What false ideas tend to cancel out these powerful blessings?

PART 3

Experiences that Seek to Extinguish

Chapter 15

LIMITED LOVE

*I*t pains me to write Part 3 of this book because of the anguish many people experience due to the people in their lives who should love them, but don't. At times, just the thought of all the injustice and unkindness in this world brings me to tears, and if we really knew; that is to say, if we had God's view of each individual's breaking heart, none of us could ever endure it.

Having no desire to push anyone over the edge with disheartening thoughts, let me first educate and encourage you that God is neither the author of the hatred on the earth, nor is He "allowing" evil for some divine purpose.

Listen, please. God is love. He does not cause evil nor does He allow it to happen. On the contrary, God abhors evil. He hears the cries of those who are being oppressed and has great compassion for them.

Then, why doesn't God stop evil from happening? This is a question which deserves an answer which is seldom taught correctly. You may have never heard the opposite of this before, so brace yourself.

❧ God is NOT in control of everything that happens on the earth. ❧

You might find this a shocking statement because in the body of Christ today the expression, "God is sovereign," gets tossed about as the answer to any question we can't answer.

Perhaps you strongly disagree, but I encourage you to look in a Strong's concordance for the words "sovereign" and "sovereignty." You will be surprised what you find (or don't).

I declare to you with total confidence that things do happen every minute of every day that are **not** God's will. The examples are too numerous to include, but here is a principle one.

> **2 Peter 3:9**
> *The Lord is not slack concerning His promise, as some count slackness, but is longsuffering toward us, not willing that any should perish but that all should come to repentance.*

God is not willing that anyone should perish, but that all will come to repentance; however, every single day people die refusing to believe in the One whom God sent to save them from perishing. God wants them to turn to Him and find life, but **they** reject the One who loves them and died to save them. Why doesn't God do something about this?

There is a higher principle at work which God in His sovereignty has put in place in eternity past. God has given each living being choice. We are not puppets on strings being moved about at the whim of God. We have volition. God has provided the path to life, but we have the ability to accept or reject that gift. He **can't** force people to receive Him because He has set in place the principle of choice. One could say God *sovereignly* determined mankind would have choice, but we cannot say the choices people make are in any way His sovereign will.

Everyone has a free will. That is why bad things happen to both good and bad people. Day after day, people make selfish and damaging choices—their *own* choices. Those decisions usually end up harming someone else. We must not blame God for the wrong choices of others.

Did you know even angels have choice? All the angels in heaven and on earth at this moment are choosing to love and obey God. They aren't robots or slaves. They choose. We know this to be true because the enemy was once an angel of God, and he determined to exalt himself above God who justly cast him out of heaven along with one-third of the angels who chose to follow him.

Thankfully, God further devastated him at the cross dis-arming Him (Heb. 2:14-15, Col. 2:15). Those who believe in Jesus do not need to fear the enemy. We have every right to believe God will protect us from the enemy's attempts to harm us. Our part is to believe God and not the devil for he is still roaming the earth seeking to steal, kill, and destroy. We are to resist him in Jesus' name.

Bad Examples

Many of us know the pain of having one or more parents who fell short of demonstrating God's love to us. Imperfection and even deliberate abuse from parent to child can rob a child of security and the knowledge of God's love for them.

Is God to blame for this? No. Parents are to blame. Some of them were also unloved by their own parents, and instead of choosing to break the cycle of withholding love, ended up behaving as they were treated.

Sadly, this chain of pain can go on many generations before someone says, "No! This stops here and now. I am not going to behave as my parents did toward me. I will not let my children feel unloved. I am going to show my kids God's love for them as I am learning for myself how much He loves me."

I remember sitting numb in church one day after the teaching ended. The sermon was a beautiful one about how God loves us like a father. Glorious examples had been given to help us all see how lovely it is to be His children, and that we can confidently come before Him as a child confidently approaches his own dad. People were coming to the altar in tears obviously touched by this teaching. What was wrong with me? Why did I feel so unaffected?

Over time it became obvious to me why my emotions were flat. My father fell woefully short of being a good father to me. My heart wasn't connecting with the idea God was like a father. My husband, who preached the message while fighting off tears, was the complete opposite. His dad was a fantastic father to him. My dad was cruel with his words. His father was encouraging and proud of him. My father never complimented me. David felt like his dad knew him. My dad didn't know me and didn't seem interested in knowing me. Dave's dad offered wise counsel. My father usually gave harsh digging criticism. No wonder my heart could not respond to the idea of God loving me like *my* father.

Every year, when Father's Day approached, love and duty sent me to the store to buy a Father's Day card. Reading the glowing testimonies of how much someone might feel loved by one's father, brought tears to my eyes every time. I wanted so much to be able to say these things about my dad, but I could not select those cards in a good conscience. I would keep looking until I found one that neither spoke eloquently of my dad nor was unkind. Then I would write my father a neutral happy Father's Day greeting and put the card in the mail. How I loved my daddy. How I longed for him to love me back.

All little girls
Deify their daddies
And caring fathers
Do not disappoint them.
Even when with maturity
She realizes his humanity
There grows an acceptance
Because love is there.

Daddy…
What does it feel like?
It must be warm and cuddly,
Possibly a place to rest,
Maybe a safe retreat,
Perhaps a non-condemning
Helping hand extended.

Oh, for one sincere
Word of praise,
One small

Show of affection,
One morsel of caring!
It would sustain me
For a lifetime. [33]

Over time, this truth has been observable in the lives of many people we've met. Friends and family members who were sincerely loved by their fathers have a clearer confidence in life and believing God loves them as their Father is as easy as breathing.

For many of us, God's love is more rightly *contrasted* to an earthly father's than compared. We need to believe God loves us and His fatherly love is pure and wonderful. Even though the human comparison doesn't work for some personally, we can come to a place where we can happily say God is our Father without cringing.

Whatever our own fathers lacked, we learn God's love supplies. God encourages. God loves without condition. He knows us and actually likes us. Instead of lamenting we don't have a father who loved us as he should have, we can choose to rejoice we now have a Father who will love us always.

When I was seven years old
My daddy told my mom,
"I don't love you anymore,
Good-bye. I'm gone."
And he never asked what I thought
Then out the door he flew,
And he never really was my daddy again.

But Father, you've been the Daddy
Daddy refused to be.
You took me in your arms
And then you bounced me on Your knee.
And You taught me all the good things

---

[33] "Oh, for One Morsel of Caring," part of a poem by C. D. Hildebrand, 1989

A daddy really should.
God, you filled the emptiness
In me.[34]

As a young adult, I came to a time when I had nothing but disdain for my father. He didn't seem to want anything to do with me, so I returned the sentiment. He purposely caused me so much grief over my lifetime that I stopped trying to gain his affection. I'm not proud of this. I was wrong to hate him.

Thankfully, one day while I was praying, God encouraged me to forgive my father and to love him and stay in communication with him even though doing so set me up for further frustrations and disappointments. God gave me a sincere love and compassion for my daddy and the grace to "love him anyway."

Over time, my father also learned to love me in his own stifled way. I don't remember him ever saying he loved me, but one of the times when I told him I loved him, shortly before he passed away, he said, "Me too," and I knew that he was sincere. That would have to be enough. The last time I saw him, we departed in peace with that same old familiar disconnected awkward hug. Some of you don't have even that, and I'm so sorry.

❧ Please don't let your past destroy your future. ❧

I've used this example of God as our Father, but the truth is when anyone who is supposed to love us doesn't love us, it can cause so much pain and interfere with our knowledge and belief in God's love for us personally. (Often, we are not even aware this is happening.) When your own mother rejects you it's normal to wonder if God accepts you or if He isn't just as disgusted with you as your mom seems to be. When your spouse is harsh and critical and withholds affection even knowing how much it would mean to you, you might think God

---

[34] "God, You Are My Family", part of a song by C. D. Hildebrand, circa 1990

is the same way. Divorce can leave a spouse wondering if God might abandon him also.

Please know God is not behind any of the horrible things we experience at the hands of those who should be loving us unconditionally. His heart is breaking when He sees our pain and longs to heal us and bring us peace and the joy of knowing He loves us even when no one else does. **We are valuable to Him.** We are precious to Him. He loves us even if, quite frankly, everything people say about us *is* true—even if we *are* horrible, God deeply loves us and is working in our hearts right now to show His love for us. Amazingly, God loves us even if *we* are the person who has failed to love those we should. That is how amazing His love is.

"Lord, help those who are right now struggling with any rela-tionship that is in disrepair. Bring forgiveness and resolution between family members and friends. Heal the damage that has been done to us. Teach us how greatly we are loved and forgiven so we may also love and forgive. Help us to endure imperfect love from those who surround us and to turn to You as the only source of absolute love."

"The Spirit of the Lord God is upon Me,
Because the Lord has anointed Me
To preach good tidings to the poor;
He has sent Me to **heal the brokenhearted**,
To proclaim liberty to the **captives**,
And the opening of the prison to those who are **bound**;
² To proclaim the acceptable year of the Lord,
And the day of vengeance of our God;
To comfort all who mourn,
³ To **console** *those who mourn in Zion,*
To give them **beauty** *for ashes,*
The oil of **joy** *for mourning,*
The garment of **praise** *for the spirit of heaviness;*
That they may be called trees of righteousness,
The planting of the Lord, that He may be glorified."
Isaiah 61:1-3

Continuing the Journey

As I was editing this chapter, I broke down in tears thinking of all the people who are hurting because they do not feel loved. I know how horrible it feels and how much damage it causes. May the Lord comfort you and heal the devastating effects you might be experiencing. Please know God will indeed heal your broken heart and make you whole. He will bring you peace. He will come and rescue you from the devastation left behind by those who fail to love as they should.

1. Read the above passage again. Do you see yourself in this passage? Express your faith that Jesus has come to minister to you personally.

2. Consider verse 3. This is God's goal for us—that the pain and rejection we might have felt in life can not only be healed but replaced with joy and dancing. Have you experienced this healing? If so, in what ways?

A Personal Note

One of the ways God healed me of not knowing the love of a father was through watching my husband love our children. Each day, he loved them unconditionally. As our children turned into teenagers, my husband told each one of them personally, "There is nothing you can do that would make me not love you. Nothing." This is the heart of God for us.

⊱ **May the Lord replace your tears with joy.** ⊰

Chapter 16

ABUSIVE "LOVE"

*I*t is not possible to understand why people purposely hurt others, especially when they damage their own flesh and blood. Yet all around us are those who are broken. Let us be aware of this so we may show kindness to all.

Inconsistent Love

Inconsistent love is very confusing. One day you feel someone loves you unconditionally, but the next day you feel rejected for no apparent reason. Sometimes what you say is received graciously and then another day, you face harsh criticism. You get to the point where you are always walking on pins and needles when you are around this person because you never know what is going to trigger a negative response.

Someone who has experienced inconsistent love can develop insecurities around other people and even begin to view God as overly sensitive. This can negatively affect our ability to trust in new relationships and in God.

Thankfully, God's love is steadfast. He isn't moody toward us at all. This is one of the biggest contrasts about God's love and human love. Human love can be crushing and confusing due to its inconsistencies. He doesn't kick us when we're down for the count. God's love is steady and sure and seeks to build us up.

Matthew 12:20
A bruised reed He will not break,
And smoking flax He will not quench.

Self-Centered "Love"

Nothing is more pure and tender than a mother's love, unless your mother was self-centered (or father, or spouse, or sibling, or friend). There is a whole generation today who grew up with a single focus—self. They were trained to be this way by well-meaning adults who taught self-realization as the single most important goal in life. Then, these egocentric children have children. This will either snap someone out of self-centeredness or tragically, children will be viewed as obstacles to the parents' happiness—an inconvenience. The child, of course, feels this.

Have you ever heard the expression, "Happy wife, happy life"? We can take this expression two ways. Perhaps the husband wants to make his wife happy, so he does those things he knows will please her. That is a positive sentiment and likely brings joy to his wife. Often however, what people mean is if they don't give their wife what she wants, there will be negative consequences to endure. This is not a healthy relationship.

The self-centered person is never truly happy. When others don't try to satisfy his every whim, he can get angry and resentful which makes for a very frustrating relationship.

What is the answer? It's simple: Jesus-centeredness. When we focus on Jesus, we begin to feel His heart of love for others. When we focus on Jesus, we also find forgiveness for those whose selfish tendencies are causing us emotional damage. When we begin to lay down our lives for those whom God has called us to love, life happens in them and in us. Keep your eyes on Jesus.

Abusive "Love"

Nothing is more evil than taking advantage of a child. More people than will ever admit, experienced some sort of sexual impropriety growing up. If this happened to them by a parent, their psyche can be severely damaged. Imagine how the statement, "God is like your father," might sound to someone who was physically abused by a father.

God is not like an abusive parent in any way at all. If you, like so many others were abused as a child, God cares and wants to heal you. Yes, *heal* you. He will even remove the pain your memories cause. He is this powerful!

He will heal the devastating effects these abuses caused. It will take some time, but God will replace the emptiness these experiences provoked, and fill you with the knowledge of His good and pure love so much so that you will be able to forgive the offender.

It is also important to remember God does not cause or allow abuse. The offender is the one who is to blame.

"Jesus, help us to forgive those who abused us. Help us to love them as You have loved us. Help us not to repeat the damage done toward us with those You call us to love. Because You love us, we are supernaturally able to love others. Thank-You for healing our pain and making us whole."

> *I waited patiently for the Lord;*
> *And He inclined to me,*
> *And heard my cry.*
> *² He also brought me up out of a horrible pit,*
> *Out of the miry clay,*
> *And set my feet upon a rock,*
> *And established my steps.*
> *³ He has put a new song in my mouth—*
> *Praise to our God;*
> *Many will see it and fear,*
> *And will trust in the Lord.*

Psalm 40:1-3

Continuing the Journey

1. How might the Psalm above speak to the heart of someone who has experienced abusive "love"?

2. Often, in an effort to be "authentic" we might share with a group the intimate details of abuse against us. Why might this not be wise? On the other hand, if you feel the need to discuss such matters with someone, make sure it is with a trusted friend or confidential professional.

3. Keeping the above question in mind, share about how inconsistent, abusive, and self-centered love can damage someone and negatively affect one's ability to know he is loved by God. How can understanding these effects help us be better parents, etc.?

Chapter 17

REJECTION

---

1 John 3:1-2
Behold what manner of love the Father has bestowed on us, that we should be called children of God! Therefore the world does not know us, because it did not know Him. ²Beloved, now we are children of God; and it has not yet been revealed what we shall be, but we know that when He is revealed, we shall be like Him, for we shall see Him as He is.

So great a love has been given to us. So great, that we are now His very own children. Since the world rejects God, they don't see how special we are to Him. In fact, increasingly, the world despises us for our faith to the point of thinking we are mentally unstable for believing in what we cannot see.

As His sons and daughters we are destined to be like Him when He is revealed. No longer will we see Him as "through a glass dimly," but we will see Him face to face. The word "see" in verse 2 in the Greek is much more than the physical act of looking or observing. It means, "to gaze (that is, with wide open eyes, as at something remarkable)."[35]

Even knowing they are accepted by God to this degree, many Christians still battle feelings of rejection by God because

---

[35] Strong's Concordance

they were rejected in life in some way. People who were adopted, for example, often experience emptiness knowing their parents gave them away. If the home where they are adopted is a loving and kind home where they are accepted and nurtured, the pain of the rejection is lessoned, but sadly, this is not always the case.

Others accumulate the fear of rejection through negative life experiences that tend to wear a person down—not being accepted by friends at school, being ill-treated by teachers, having a visible mental or physical imperfection—too tall, too short, too thin, too fat, too young, too old, bad dating experiences, difficulties finding employment, discrimination, unkindness by a trusted friend, divorce, and let us not forget the constant lies that seek to steal our confidence.

What we all need to know is that except for a very few individuals who were raised in the perfect home with the perfect parents and adoring siblings, and great friends, who manage to be successful in every way, advance in their careers, meet the perfect mate who treats them lovingly every day—and on and on, there are very few people left with reasons to feel completely secure.

Everyone, including those we might consider perfect, at some time in their lives will face rejection. So, in a real way, we can all find ways to understand each other. Perhaps someone might not understand exactly how not having a father who loved as he should have, would cause someone to feel insecurities about God's love, but maybe that same person experienced the pain of rejection by a spouse abandoning him. Or, having been betrayed by a dear and close friend, someone else might understand someone's pain from a divorce. These situations, though different, all involve rejection. Having experienced the comfort of God in these circumstances, we are able to encourage each other.

God understands the pain of rejection even more than we ourselves. He created Adam and Eve—gave them all they could ever need, but they chose to believe Satan's word more than His. Still He provided for them because He loved them. The Children of Israel were miraculously led out of bondage *through* the Red Sea, mind you! Before you know it, they are giving glory to a golden calf! Still, God's love for them did not cease.

The greatest example is, of course, that God gave His only Son to die for us to give us everlasting life. Jesus was ridiculed, beaten and crucified by the very ones He came to save. They rejected their own Messiah, and the world continues to reject His love today.

> ### Isaiah 53:3-5
> *He is despised and rejected by men,*
> *A Man of sorrows and acquainted with grief.*
> *And we hid, as it were, our faces from Him;*
> *He was despised, and we did not esteem Him.*
> *⁴ Surely He has borne our griefs*
> *And carried our sorrows;*
> *Yet we esteemed Him stricken,*
> *Smitten by God, and afflicted.*
> *⁵ But He was wounded for our transgressions,*
> *He was bruised for our iniquities;*
> *The chastisement for our peace was upon Him,*
> *And by His stripes we are healed.*

The remedy for rejection is found in knowing we have a God who understands. He overcame rejection by forgiving those who were refusing Him. That same ability to forgive resides in every believer. No doubt, you have been rejected in some way during your life. Perhaps you feel worthless because no one on earth has ever seemed to see anything of worth in you, but consider this:

❧ God sees you and treasures you, ❧
enough to give His life for you—

This is not meant to minimize the damage you suffered, only to assure you there is healing for us from our Father who does love us. As we begin to understand how greatly we are loved and accepted by God, we are able to heal and gain confidence in that love. Yes, it is likely another situation will arise when rejection once again stings us, but as we turn to Him, we will be healed again.

> ### Ephesians 1:3-6
> *Blessed be the God and Father of our Lord Jesus Christ, who has blessed us with every spiritual blessing in the heavenly places in Christ, ⁴ just as He chose us in Him before the foundation of the world, that we should be holy and without blame before Him in love, ⁵ having predestined us to adoption as sons by Jesus Christ to Himself, according to the good pleasure of His will, ⁶ to the praise of the glory of His grace, by which* **He made us accepted in the Beloved***.*

Earthly relationships will fail us, but Jesus never will. We are His people. We are His friends. AND we are His children— having been adopted by the living God. Instead of the constant nagging insecurities brought on by rejection, we can now live as those who are accepted in the Beloved. God accepts you into His love—just as you are.

"Father, thank-You for accepting us. Thank-You for healing the pain of rejection by those who should have accepted us. Thank-You for making us whole. Thank-You for loving each one of us personally."

> *Although my father and my mother*
> *have abandoned me,*
> *Yet the Lord will take me up*
> *[adopt me as His child].*
>
> *Psalm 27:10 AMP*

Continuing the Journey

1. What rejections have you faced in life?

2. Did these experiences hinder you from feeling loved by God? If so, explain in what ways. If not, explain why not?

3. Why is it that knowing we are God's accepted and beloved children help us overcome the devastations of rejection?

4. In what ways will forgiveness toward our offenders set us free from the fear of rejection?

Chapter 18

WHEN LIFE WEARS US DOWN

John 16:33
*"These things I have spoken to you, that in
Me you may have peace. In the world you will
have tribulation; but be of good cheer, I have
overcome the world,"*

Everyone experiences difficulties in life—even those who put their faith in Jesus Christ; or perhaps it's better to say, *especially* believers in Jesus Christ.

2 Timothy 3:12
*Yes, and all who desire to live godly in Christ
Jesus will suffer persecution.*

It is because we align ourselves with Jesus and desire to live a godly life that the world opposes us. John wrote, "Therefore, the world does not know us, because it did not know Him," (1 Jn. 3:1). So, we should not be surprised when the world or those claiming to be Christians, persecute us.

Many of our difficulties, though, have almost nothing to do with our faith—simply due to the fact we live on this earth in mortal bodies are reason enough. We want to be at peace with everyone, and we take steps toward that goal, but not everyone returns the same grace. We all know snarly people who seem determined to make everyone around them miserable. Sure, we can ignore many people in life, but it's very difficult to over-look members of our own family—our parents, our spouse, and children who sometimes cause grief.

There are so many things in life that can bring us down—betrayal by a trusted friend, pressures at work, struggling to make ends meet, depression, medical issues, and feeling trapped in life.

Furthermore, tragedies happen such as weather events, deaths of those we love, and political unrest. We feel shaken and even alone as we grapple to survive. Then there is failure. Being disappointed with one's self is very difficult to bear.

The truth is everyone goes through trying times in life, and most of us face experiences that seem impossible to bear. Pessimists expect them, and optimists are often surprised by them, but no one in their right mind enjoys suffering especially not long-term. It is a fact of this "life" as we exist in this current world where chaos and tragedy happen and people fall increasingly short of respecting each other.

> ### 2 Timothy 3:1-7
> *But know this, that in the last days perilous times will come: ² For men will be lovers of themselves, lovers of money, boasters, proud, blasphemers, disobedient to parents, unthankful, unholy, ³ unloving, unforgiving, slanderers, without self-control, brutal, despisers of good, ⁴ traitors, headstrong, haughty, lovers of pleasure rather than lovers of God, ⁵ having a form of godliness but denying its power. And from such people turn away! ⁶ For of this sort are those who creep into households and make captives of gullible women loaded down with sins, led away by various lusts, ⁷ always learning and never able to come to the knowledge of the truth.*

Evil and selfish people always abound, but Paul wrote it would get worse in the last days. This world is a tough place, and some of its inhabitants are not pleasant, so on top of "life" that can be difficult at times, we have to deal with people who greatly fall short of the glory of God. We can develop the perspective that everything and everyone are against us. We can begin to think God is as callous as those around us, and we ourselves can become hardened.

Matthew 24:12
And because lawlessness will abound, the love of many will grow cold.

Difficult times and unpleasant people are part of this life. The wonderful news is, God is not our enemy. Instead, He is always **for** us, even when we or others are not perfect. He is not sending difficult times and challenging people into our lives to teach us some celestial lesson or to punish us for our weaknesses. He knows how to speak to us directly. God comforts us as we face difficulties. Not only that, He is working all things together for our good. He *died* for us! He is not condemning us. He is sticking up for us in the face of our accusers.

Romans 8:33-34
Who shall bring a charge against God's elect? It is God who justifies. ³⁴ Who is he who condemns? It is Christ who died, and furthermore is also risen, who is even at the right hand of God, who also makes intercession for us.

Christians have a certain advantage in this life. When the world goes through hard times, they tend to grow bitter. We, however, as children of God grow better (Rom.5:1-4). So, it isn't that when we come to Jesus we never face difficult circumstances, but it is true that no matter what happens, God is working on our side to work it for our good. God is not causing evil in our lives, rather He is perfectly capable of making it work for our good.

When We Wear Ourselves Down

No matter how much we don't love ourselves at times, we need to remember God does love us, and He knows us best. When we are tempted to focus on our weaknesses, shortcomings, and failures, let us remember God sees us right now and loves us right now and He is working in us to bring us where He wants us to be.

When you feel worthless, remember He values you enough to give His Son to die for you. He's not mad at us for feeling insecure or being flawed. No matter how bad life gets, we can overcome anything when we know and believe in His exceedingly great and undeserved love for us.

"Jesus, sometimes it feels like everyone and everything are against us. Thank-You so much that You are always for us. In every situation, remind us to focus on Your love and Your power and Your goodness, and not on the wind and waves that come our way. Instead of blaming You for hard times, help us turn to You for help knowing fully that You are NOT to blame and You are in us and will work all things together for our good. Thank-You for making us better persons as we go through difficult times. Help us to rest in Your love for us when it seems no one else on earth loves us."

For as high as the heavens are above the earth,
So great is His lovingkindness toward those who fear Him.
¹² As far as the east is from the west,
So far has He removed our transgressions from us.
¹³ Just as a father has compassion on his children,
So the Lord has compassion on those who fear Him.
¹⁴ For He Himself knows our frame;
He is mindful that we are but dust.

Psalm 103:11-14
NASB

Continuing the Journey

1. Before you knew Jesus, what was your usual response when hard times happened?

2. Why is it we should not take personally many of the things that happen in this life?

3. Sometimes, it IS personal. Either the enemy is directly attacking us, or people are. This can be very painful. What scriptures can help us remember God loves us and is not working against us?

4. What role do you think grace and faith play in believing in God's love even when life gets us down?

5. In what ways can we respond differently to difficult times and people when we know we are loved by our God?

Chapter 19

UNREALISTIC SOCIETAL EXPECTATIONS

---

*H*ere in the United States of America and in many other societies, high standards are set for our citizens. These are not always written down in one place nor are they legally required. They are gradually accumulated as someone grows up and is exposed to cultural peer pressure. One might observe them overtly in educational ads or more subtly in entertainment and advertisement media, and sadly, we often encounter these norms in painful personal ways.

Physical Appearance

Let me first address physical appearance since this is one of the most prevalent ways in which people are judged by society.

If you go to any public place and just observe the people who are there, it will be very difficult to find many "perfect" people. You will find individuals of all heights, weights, ages, and manner of dress. You will see people who in no way measure up to perfection—not at all. Most people do not look like a Hollywood star or a professional athlete. Most people just look like a relative or friend you know and love even though they are not the most beautiful person on earth.

When we observe what real people look like, we realize almost no one fits the world's standards of perfection. Most of us are too short, too tall, too fat, too thin, too young, too old, out of shape, ill-shaped, or have hair that doesn't cooperate or is thinning. We grow old, and apart from surgery most people can't afford, we get wrinkles. This is not fair, but it's true for all.

We can know this, but still be at odds with what we see in the mirror each day. We can develop the idea we have less value than someone who is more beautiful than we are. People we encounter during the day sometimes might even make their negative appraisal of us obvious, by staring in disgust or making a derogatory comment.

The world's evaluation of us hurts. It is unfair. It is unkind. We must not, though, allow the uninformed evaluations of us by others, prevent us from believing God loves us just as we are, nor should we permit these negative reviews to keep us from pursuing what God is calling us to do.

You see, God is not impressed by people's good looks. He loves ALL of us equally. Yes, we might not fit any description of perfection, but God is looking at our hearts, not our bodies.

1 Samuel 16:7
But the Lord said to Samuel, "Do not look at his appearance or at his physical stature, because I have refused him. For the Lord does not see as man sees; for man looks at the outward appearance, but the Lord looks at the heart."

When we are with confident and cheerful people, we forget they are not perfect-looking. We get to know them for who they are and forget about their physical flaws. We begin to see them as God sees them. On the other hand, we often meet people who seem perfect in every way, but as we get to know them more personally, we realize that they are struggling with insecurities no one sees or that their personalities are in need of some development.

God sees the real you, and that is the person He created at birth and then recreated in Christ. He will not base His will for your life on your appearance. Knowing and believing God loves us gives us confidence and joy.

> **2 Corinthians 5:16**
> *Therefore, from now on, we regard no one according to the flesh. Even though we have known Christ according to the flesh, yet now we know Him thus no longer.*

Educational Achievements

Our children did not discover going to college[36] was optional until they were in high school, and most likely they figured this out for themselves. When we talked about what was coming up next educationally, we never told them they had an option to do something different. They grew up thinking it was the normal course of one's life to go from high school to college.

Of course, we knew and accepted that eventually it would be their decision, but when that time came, our stipulation to continue living at home, was that they needed to either work full-time, attend a training school, or go to college. All our children eventually decided to attend universities and graduated in four years or less.

"Where did you go to college?" is not an uncommon question, and in certain circles the answer might determine someone's opinion of you. If you went to an expensive prestigious university, people will be impressed. If you went to a community college or lesser known university, they might think less of you. It is assumed someone who has not attended college is less intelligent which, of course, is not true. However, college really is not for everyone. There are so many careers that don't require it. An individual might be able to meet his goals in a variety of paths, and each of these should be congratulated.

God isn't evaluating us in this way at all. He made each one of us uniquely. This is to say, some of us will have a natural inclination to seek higher education, and others will want to get

---

[36] In the USA, college comes after high school, the 12th grade.

right to work. God is looking at our hearts. We do not need to feel pressured to conform to the world's standards.

Economic and Social Status

This will likely never be remedied, but it is important we review this. The poorest person who lives in a house made of cardboard and metal scraps is just as loved by God as one living in a mansion. Both individuals have value, and in Christ, both are equal.

In some cultures, you are *born* into your social class and it is nearly impossible to escape it. In my country, we have opportunity to shape our destinies and to pursue happiness. Even though this is true, social classes still exist in the U.S.A. It's just a fact of this world that certain ones will think themselves superior to others, and this can work both ways. A poor person might despise the rich equally as much as a rich person might look down on the poor. However, in the body of Christ, we are to love as brethren.

During the time of the Early Church, someone who was in debt with another might need to become that person's servant to pay off the debt. Both the borrower and lender were equal in Christ and were to treat each other with respect. It wasn't uncommon for a person of lesser economic success to become an elder in the church. He was treated with the respect due him, even by the rich. We are not to despise the poor, but rather minister to them. Nor are we to despise the rich.

2 Corinthians 8:8-9, 13-15
I speak not by commandment, but I am testing the sincerity of your love by the diligence of others. ⁹ For you know the grace of our Lord Jesus Christ, that though He was rich, yet for your sakes He became poor, that you through His poverty might become rich… ¹³ For I do not mean that others should be eased and you burdened; ¹⁴ but by an equality, that now at this time your abundance may supply their

> *lack, that their abundance also may supply your lack—that there may be equality. ¹⁵ As it is written, "He who gathered much had nothing left over, and he who gathered little had no lack."*

Jesus was not forced to humble Himself and live as a human being. He could easily have arrived on horse-drawn chariots decorated with gold and jewels. Instead, He became poor in that being God, He became man, so we could receive "all things pertaining to life and godliness."

> **Philippians 2:3-8**
> *Let nothing be done through selfish ambition or conceit, but in lowliness of mind let each esteem others better than himself. ⁴ Let each of you look out not only for his own interests, but also for the interests of others. ⁵ Let this mind be in you which was also in Christ Jesus, ⁶ who, being in the form of God, did not consider it robbery to be equal with God, ⁷ but made Himself of no reputation, taking the form of a bondservant, and coming in the likeness of men. ⁸ And being found in appearance as a man, He humbled Himself and became obedient to the point of death, even the death of the cross.*

Accomplishments and Experiences

Consider the multi-faceted ways we evaluate each other based on our experiences. When we meet each other for the first time, we might ask some of these questions (or simply wonder about them). Are you married? Divorced? Do you have children? Grandchildren? How many? Where do you live? In what sports do you participate? Do you keep yourself in shape? Where have you traveled? What books do you read? Whom do you know? What degrees did you earn? What is your profession? Are you successful in your career? What talents do you possess? What is your political affiliation?

In the church, your status will likely be determined by how long you've been a Christian, if you went to Bible College, if you earned an MDiv or Doctorate, what musical talents you possess, how "dedicated" you are, how much you give, ministries you lead, if your children are "serving the Lord" or not, and on and on.

While it is true Christians tend to excel at what they set themselves to do, it isn't true any one of us is better than the other based on our accomplishments or experiences. We have friends who travel all over the world for their ministries. Others feel keenly called to minister locally. Some possess high academic degrees. Others have none. Some enjoy dedicating themselves to service within the church, others are serving Him in their homes and communities. One is not superior to the other. Let each person serve God as He has given us grace. God's love for us is not measured out based on our accomplishments.

Manufactured Challenges

Agree with me or not on this, but for quite some time, a concern has been growing in my heart. Increasingly, there is a tendency to engage in extreme activities, and we are giving much esteem to those who accomplish physically challenging or dangerous goals.

For example, people who are very much "into" their health sometimes engage in activities which are in no way healthy. They push their bodies to extremes and risk their lives and health while touting physical fitness often ending up with injuries or death. This is not meant to judge anyone who sets a goal for himself; goals can be healthy, but a whole new culture has formed around it and the bragging rights come as each experience is undertaken.

We see this also within the church with activities such as doing a 40-day fast or visiting dangerous regions for ministry. We can't know the motivations for individuals engaging in such experiences, but we shouldn't feel pressured into doing something we don't feel called to do.

God isn't asking us to go on a 40-day fast. The very few examples of this in the Bible were God-ordained. Yet some of the teachings we heard in our youth clearly implied that almost every believer should at one time in their lives do a forty day fast. This simply is not true, and it is a dangerous standard to hold up to others. We know the disciples fasted from time to time because it is recorded in the book of Acts, but did you know that no epistle writer ever instructed the people to fast? There is certainly nothing wrong with fasting, but it isn't required.

May these truths set you free to be who God has called you to be and do what He is enabling you to do. Remember, God is looking at your faith, not your accomplishments.

God's Perspective of You

Take a deep breath. Hold it. Exhale slowly. Relax a little while. Remember God loves you more than you will ever be able to experience. What matters to Him most of all is you know and believe He loves you. This is your first love He wants you to always cherish and enjoy. When you feel stressed out about not meeting the world's or church's standards for beauty or status, recognize God is looking at the real you. Each day you are being transformed into His image as you keep your focus on Jesus. Do your best to look your best and be your best, but don't permit what others think determine your worth or cause you to think God loves you less or to keep you from fulfilling His calling on your life.

"Father, help us to see that the only person's view of us that matters is Yours. When we look in the mirror, let us see Jesus as You transform us from within. Help us not to be hindered from knowing how greatly You love us by anyone else's opinion of us nor by our own negative opinions of ourselves."

154

*You are His workmanship
created in Christ Jesus for good works
which God prepared beforehand
that you should walk in them.*

Ephesians 2:10

Continuing the Journey

1. In what ways have you felt inferior or superior based on the world's standards?

2. Have you ever allowed a perceived inferiority to keep you from doing what you'd like? If not, how have you over-come in this area?

3. Do you feel you need to over-compensate for your sup-posed insufficiencies?

4. In what ways can knowing and believing God loves us, free us to be the people He has called us to be even if we are not perfect?

Chapter 20

LONG-TERM STRUGGLES

When we face situations that seem to go on forever and it seems our prayers are not being answered, we can, quite naturally, grow weary. When we experience physical pain or weakness for months, and even years, we will be tempted to think God is withholding the answers we need. This can weigh down our hearts and challenge our faith in our loving God.

Even if we are overcoming these accusations against our Father who loves us, and continue to believe in His promises, the process of dealing with long-term undesirable circumstances is exhausting often leaving us physically drained and mentally fatigued. We can experience frustration, depression, and be tempted to give up hope. If we aren't careful, we can focus so much on our situations which are reasonably demanding our attention, that we forget to remember God loves us and is with us while we go through them.

Overcoming the Overwhelming

How do we find the faith we need to be victorious in the areas of our lives which seem resistant to our efforts and prayers? Do we simply accept what appears to be the hand we've been dealt, or do we look to our loving God who promises to help us even in the face of impossibilities?

First, it is important to understand God loves us "in sickness and in health." He isn't angry with us for being sick or struggling in other areas; no, not at all. While we might be tempted to throw in the towel, God will never give up on us. Instead, He is working in us to give us wisdom and strengthen our faith. What incredible rest we find when we understand this truth.

God IS Willing

Most Christians take Jesus at His word when He said nothing is impossible for God. In other words, we believe God is *able*. He is God after all; and if He, God Almighty, says nothing is impossible to those who believe, then nothing is impossible to us.

Where we sometimes get confused is with the under-standing of God's *willingness* to help us.

> **1 John 5:14-15**
> *Now this is the confidence that we have in Him,*
> *that if we ask anything **according to His will**,*
> *He hears us. [15] And if we know that He hears*
> *us, **whatever** we ask, we **know** that we have*
> *the petitions that we have asked of Him.*

When we ask God for something He is willing to do, then logically He hears us and gives us whatever we ask of Him. "Whatever"—don't you love words like that?

> **Matthew 21:22**
> *And **whatever** things you ask in prayer,*
> *believing, you will receive."*
> **John 14:13**
> *And **whatever** you ask in My name, that I will*
> *do, that the Father may be glorified in the Son.*

The knowledge of His will is revealed to us both in the written word and in our spirits which, of course, will never con-tradict what is written. Perhaps the clearest demonstration of the will of God can be observed in the life of Christ.

Mark 1:40-42
Now a leper came to Him, imploring Him, kneeling down to Him and saying to Him, "__If You are willing__, You can make me clean."
41 Then Jesus, moved with compassion, stretched out His hand and touched him, and said to him, "I am willing; be cleansed."
42 As soon as He had spoken, immediately the leprosy left him, and he was cleansed.

Jesus came to earth to reveal the Father and His will. His life on earth was His way of saying, "Look everyone at the great love I have for you!" We see Jesus teaching His disciples, lovingly preparing them for the kingdom that was soon to come, feeding the thousands, healing the multitudes, associating with the outcasts, and laying down His life. The only people He opposed were the proud and self-righteous. The good news is, God isn't doing battle with His beloved children. He is working constantly for our good to give to us all we need.

Romans 8:31
If God is for us, who can be against us?

God is not some inadequate communicator who must use primitive methods to speak to His children. We have a **relationship** with Him. We are His sheep and hear His voice. He speaks to our hearts directly and clearly. He is leading us by His Spirit, not by circumstances. He will comfort us, give us wisdom, show us His will, and answer our prayers. Yes, He will indeed speak to us when we face various trials, but He isn't sending them as some sort of malicious message.

Furthermore, He is also NOT ever going to make someone *else* suffer to teach *you* something. God forbid! Yet how many times have you heard someone imply such? Who is this barbaric maniac so many Christians believe is our God? Not only did He give His own Son up for us so that we would have life, He promises to also freely *give* us all things.

Do you think He is doling out hard times to this one and that because He can't get through to us? No! He is graciously *giving* us what we need and this includes physical, emotional, and psychological healing. He gave His life so we could be *saved*, not so we would perish. He was wounded so we could be healed in every area of our lives, not so we would be sick. ALL of this was God's way of evidently declaring to us with full assurance that He loves us! We need to pray we will profoundly believe in the goodness of God.

> **1 Peter 2:24**
> *He Himself bore our sins in His own body on the tree, that we, having died to sins, might live for righteousness—by whose stripes you were healed.*

We have a saying on our wall that reads,

> **Faith isn't believing that God can.**
> **It is knowing that He will.**

Of course God *can*—He is God, and nothing is impossible for Him. He wants to bring us to a place of confidence of knowing He *will*.

Things We Accept

It is important to share these truths repeatedly because it is so very crucial to our understanding of God's love for us. We need to know and believe God is love and His desire for us is always born out of love. Instead, without giving it much thought, we often accept the enemy's intentions and the junk the world flings in our direction *as if from God*.

God is not routinely sending us sickness during "cold and flu season." Let us not assume we will start sneezing when pollen flies. Why not rather declare that "by His wounds, we were healed"?

❧ It is not arrogance to believe in the promises and provisions of God. ❧

God wants to help us believe He is good. We do not have to accept something just because the rest of the world does. Praise be to our wonderful and faithful God.

> **Psalm 91:4-7**
> *You shall not be afraid of the terror by night,*
> *Nor of the arrow that flies by day,*
> *⁶ Nor of the pestilence that walks in darkness,*
> *Nor of the destruction that lays waste at*
> *noonday.*
> *⁷ A thousand may fall at your side,*
> **And ten thousand at your right hand;**
> **But it shall not come near you.**

We are all getting older. Our bodies fight us, but we can fight back. Yes, we know that one day we will fall asleep and forever be with Jesus, but we can refuse to assume what the world does concerning "aging." (I'm not saying we won't grow old, just that it's ok to believe God for good health.) Have you heard about the ninety-year-old grandmother who "run circles around" her children and grandchildren and who is as "sharp as a tack" mentally? That's the grandmother I am asking God to make me in the name of Jesus. According to my faith, be it unto me!

> **Deuteronomy 34:7**
> *Moses was one hundred and twenty years old*
> *when he died. His eyes were not dim nor his*
> *natural vigor diminished.*

We need to also be aware that our doctors may have a fatalistic view of aging. Everyone dies, right? Some might unconsciously accept things about getting old and dying that don't line up with what we believe or desire. They might think we are on our way out the door and begin to measure out our healthcare accordingly, but we perhaps are believing we will be satisfied with a long life.

Psalm 91:16
With long life I will satisfy him and show him
My salvation.

"I hope to live into my nineties," I tell my doctor, "So, my body needs to function at its best." She may think I'm a little crazy, but it's ok to push a bit to get the best medical care possible.

Let us not accept whatever comes our way. May we know whose child we are and how deeply we are loved by our Father.

Little Miss Joey Takes a Stand

My mom shared with me often how difficult it was being a pastor's kid when she was growing up, and David and I were determined to mitigate the potential for emotional and spiritual harm in our kids' lives. We didn't want them to resent being a PK, but rather be able to look back on it as a blessing. We also believed that having two parents was sufficient and our kids didn't need the rest of the church trying to parent them also. Most people respected the hedge of protection we subtly placed around them and simply loved them.

One Sunday morning after church, everyone was standing around in front of the church talking as we customarily did, and since the cars were parked where everyone was gathered, our daughter who was in about the first grade, innocently sat down on the hood one of the cars. To Joey, this was a completely acceptable behavior as we had an older car and didn't mind if the kids sat on it.

There was an individual in that church

161

who saw her sitting on the car and instead of informing us (we could not have been more than five steps away) took it upon himself to correct our little daughter and ordered her to get down!

Now, our kids were used to being spoken to with respect and love, even when being corrected. So, there must have been something about the manner in which this adult spoke to our daughter, a very well-mannered, polite, spunky, gregarious, confident, cheerful, and loving child, who also had a keen sense of justice that caused her to respond, "You can't tell me what to do. My daddy's the pastor," which, greatly infuriated this person who promptly took those five long steps to report our child's offense to me.

*I fought off letting out a little giggle about Joey's response (because I actually thought it was so adorable), and instead apologized and thanked the person for the information assuring him I'd speak to her. Of course, we talked to Joey about being more respectful and that sitting on other people's cars was not appropriate, but we also told her **we** were her parents and no one else had the right to boss her around. Being the sweetheart that she was, she received this correction and nothing more was said.*

*David and I were proud of our little girl for knowing who she was and we were especially touched she knew who her daddy was. If you happen to know Joella, this story will not surprise you at all. Her tender heart and strong sense of fairness is still evidenced in the ministries in which she is involved today including being a mother to five children of her own. (Don't mess with **her** kids either.)*

I share this with you to make the point that we don't have to take any bullying from the enemy or the things "life" throws at us to defeat and destroy us either. This world will criticize and falsely accuse us, but we can fight back in the name of Jesus knowing that He already won the battle for us and we can be confident in knowing who our Father is. Say this with confidence!

**I don't have to accept
the stuff this life throws my way.
∾ God is my Father! ∾**

Abraham's Faith

When facing long-term difficulties, we can look to examples of faith such as Abraham. There can be no greater example of believing God will do what He promised, even when it looks impossible.

As believers, we are not only dealing with "the facts of life"; we also have a supernatural life based in Him. This is exactly what Abraham faced. The Lord promised Abraham a son from his wife Sarah, but there were some facts screaming at him day after day, just as for some of us, our circumstances are proclaiming our problems to us. Abraham and Sarah were far too old to conceive.

> ### *Romans 4:17-21*
> *(As it is written, "I have made you a father of many nations") in the presence of Him whom he believed—God, who gives life to the dead and calls those things which do not exist as though they did; [18] who, contrary to hope, in hope believed, so that he became the father of many nations, according to what was spoken, "So shall your descendants be." [19] And not being weak in faith, he did not consider his own body, already dead (since he was about a hundred years old), and the deadness of Sarah's*

womb. 20 He did not waver at the promise of God through unbelief, but was strengthened in faith, giving glory to God, 21 and being fully convinced that what He had promised He was also able to perform.

We can be inspired by this because we also face impossibilities concerning challenging circumstances in life. We believe God has provided solutions, but the "facts" seem to speak otherwise. We need to follow Abraham's example.

It's impossible not to notice what you are experiencing or ignore the circumstances trying your faith, and it's ok to take the "facts" into consideration, but we must, "not waver at the promise of God through unbelief, but be strengthened in faith, giving glory to God be fully persuaded that what He promises He is able (and willing) to perform."

We can't simply ignore the tribulations demanding our time, energy, and money, but through it all, we can believe that the God who gives life to the dead and calls those things which do not exist as though they do, IS OUR GOD.

**⤫ I choose to trust the truth of God's promises ⤬
more than the circumstances I am facing.**

Faith Pleases God

Within the heart of every born-again believer in Jesus Christ is the desire to please God. As young adults, we thought pleasing God had to do with adhering to a very long list of dooties and don'ties which we kept as diligently as we knew how. What we didn't understand was that what actually pleases God is our faith in Him.

> **Hebrews 11:6**
> *But without faith it is impossible to please Him, for he who comes to God must believe that He is, and that He is a rewarder of those who diligently seek Him.*

When we have faith in Him, He is pleased. It is such a joy to know that when we believe God even as did Abraham, who "contrary to hope in hope believed," it pleases God. Just like anyone, I'm sure Abraham would have appreciated a more immediate fulfillment, but no matter how long the wait, he did not stop believing. This faith was "accounted to him as righteousness." Doing and don'ting doesn't make us righteous before God. Believing in Him does. When we believe in Him, we are motivated and empowered to do.

Natural Answers to Supernatural Dilemmas

God loves us so much, that He will open our eyes to solutions to our long-term struggles we can't even imagine. This is a principle we have observed that might be helpful to you which was mentioned in my second book, and here again with a new glorious example.

Often, when believing God for healing or answers to predicaments and the wait is long, it is because there exists a natural resolution we don't see yet. We see this in Paul's recommendation to Timothy to take a little wine for his stomach's sake (1 Tim. 5:23). It wasn't that God refused to heal him; it might have been the water wasn't pure enough or perhaps the wine would act as a natural medicine for what ailed him.

It makes perfect sense to me, when answers to prayer seem to be a long time in coming, for us to investigate answers which don't necessarily seem "supernatural," though the revelations of them are.

Usually, this process begins with a simple prayer requesting wisdom. Low, and behold, we hear or read something on the topic or our doctors discover we have some deficiency, and the problem is easily solved. A way to earn money we hadn't considered before becomes apparent. It's the love of God in action. He wants us to find answers to our problems, and sometimes, those solutions are within our grasp. Whether it be a growth that can be removed or the fact we are stressing a part of our body we can stop stressing or we need to supplement a vitamin or stop eating a certain food—all of this is God's help. Or, we might be facing long-term difficulties in other areas, and God sweetly speaks a solution to our hearts. We obey, and voila, the problem is solved.

Sometimes, the answer comes "accidentally." Here's a personal example. For eight years, there was a very uncomfortable localized pain in my stomach. Of course, I prayed about it, and talked to my doctors about it (we changed medical plans three times), but for some reason, no doctor took steps to see what might be causing it. I'd prayed about it, but the pain still happened often.

Recently, though, my schedule made me busier in the mornings when I usually first had a green tea to start my day and then a decaf coffee about mid-morning. It was so busy I barely got finished sipping my green tea before it was lunch time. It seemed odd to go ahead and have the decaf after lunch, so why bother? My body was just as happy with just the tea. So, for no medical reason at all, I stopped drinking coffee anticipating nothing in return.

Perhaps you've guessed it, but after about a month, I noticed it had been a very long time since the pain occurred. The only thing I'd changed was not drinking my decaf each morning. Obviously, whatever was wrong with my stomach was irritated by the coffee. Only God knows what is going on in there, but it feels like a healing to me—a pain that's been part of my life for eight years is completely gone! What a welcomed answer to prayer. Praise the Lord.

Long-term problems can wear us down and we will be tempted to think our loving and dear God has something to do with them, and He does, but ONLY in the sense He is working in our hearts and lives to bring solutions. He's right here next to us cheering us on toward victory!

"God, help those of us who are experiencing situations that are seeming to go on forever. Help us to rest in Your love especially when we grow weary. Thank-You for being right here with us in our difficulties. Thank-You for knowing what we do not know and for working everything together for our good.

God, we refuse to believe You use evil to bring about good. Life happens, and You are here with us in this life. No matter what we experience, You love us. You will never leave us or forsake us—not ever.

Father, if there is something 'natural' we can do that will help us in areas in which we struggle, we pray You will open our eyes to discover it. We put our trust in You. You are not only able to help us, but You are willing to help us. You are not only willing to help us, but You will help us. Teach us from Your word and by Your grace of all You provided and promised. Open our eyes to see and our hearts to believe.

How we praise You that simply by believing, You are pleased with us—even in the midst of the difficulties we face, You see our faith. You are smiling at us with great joy. You are proud of us for believing in You. We cry out to You in total dependence and faith. You are OUR God. You will never fail."

> *Why are you in despair, O my soul?*
> *And why are you restless and disturbed within me?*
> **Hope in God and wait expectantly for Him,**
> *for I shall again praise Him,*
> *The help of my [sad] countenance and my God.*
>
> *Psalm 43:15 AMP*

Continuing the Journey

1. Are there certain difficulties you accept? Do you know who your Daddy is?

2. Can you relate to Abraham's situation, and if so, in what ways?

3. In what ways has God helped you solve a situation by showing you a natural solution?

Chapter 21

ABUSE BY SPIRITUAL AUTHORITIES

*O*h, that this chapter didn't need to be included in the list of experiences that hinder us from knowing and believing the love God has for us. It is more widespread than we will ever know. Spiritual leaders sometimes fall terribly short of Christ's command to love. Instead they lord their authority over those whom they should be serving. It is reasonable to question whether any of these people are even believers. Jesus did say we would know them by their fruit. At the very least, they are not good shepherds.

Sexual Abuse

Our minds usually go immediately to the stories we hear on the news of young children being abused by some religious leader. Dear God, how can this ever be true within the body of Christ? How can a child comprehend God loves them when a trusted leader has sexually abused him? Can you even imagine the injured mind that emerges when these things occur? The adult spiritual authority is a representative of God! How confusing it is when God's supposed representatives behave in such a way. The perception of God's love becomes mangled and twisted.

Truly this is the worst-case scenario, and if this has happened to you, the heart of every Christian breaks for you. Rest assured, these types of acts will not go unpunished because God does not take lightly the abuse of His children.

> ### Mark 9:22
> *"But whoever causes one of these little ones who believe in Me to stumble, it would be better for him if a millstone were hung around his neck, and he were thrown into the sea."*

False Spiritual Authority

Another devastating abuse within many churches across the world concerns leaders asserting control over the lives of people within an assembly. This may happen gradually over time or be blatantly obvious upon one's first visit. It can range from a subtle type of control to overt methods.

The basic idea in a congregation such as this is that the church is a theocracy and the pastor is the ultimate spiritual authority—the last word on what is taught, and the last word on how people are managed. All will go well for attendees— *unless*—someone has the audacity to disagree with the leader's teachings or, God forbid, complain about how the pastor has dealt with someone in the church. Either quietly or publicly, this supposed offender will be alienated, not only by the pastor, but by all of those within the church who consider the pastor to be someone who cannot and must not be questioned.

Comments will be made in the shadows or even from the pulpit! Warnings will be issued to those associated with the "offender" to be careful not to associate with such troublemakers. If you get fed up with this and leave this fellowship—if they don't ask you to leave first, you will be shunned, even by your own family and people you consider to be dear friends *even if* you have been a cooperative member for many years, serving faithfully and giving consistently. Once you are no longer unquestionably loyal to that pastor, you will no longer be loved. Many times, you will not only be ignored by members of that church, but sometimes, even more drastic measures will be taken. An experience like this can be devastating to someone.

When this happens to a young person who doesn't have enough experience to assimilate what is going on, it can lead to rejecting Christianity—though likely, what is being rejected isn't Jesus. This young person can grow alienated and angry about anything that has to do with God.

The truth is, pastors are to lead, not control.

> **1 Peter 5:1-4**
> *The elders who are among you I exhort, I who am a fellow elder and a witness of the sufferings of Christ, and also a partaker of the glory that will be revealed: ² Shepherd the flock of God which is among you, serving as overseers, not by compulsion but willingly, not for dishonest gain but eagerly; ³ **nor as being lords over those entrusted to you**, but being examples to the flock; ⁴ and when the Chief Shepherd appears, you will receive the crown of glory that does not fade away.*

If you suffered at the hands of such a "pastor," try to make a distinction between such a shameful person and Jesus. Jesus loves you. He is not pressuring you with external conformity. He is lovingly working in you to be transformed from within. If you disagree with Him, He won't be surprised or offended. He will lovingly instruct you and give you a desire to follow Him.

Don't allow these false shepherds to keep you from the love of the True Shepherd. You will likely not be able to fix the problems in such an abusive system, but you can move on and continue the journey of knowing God's love for you.

The Judgment Seat of Christ

To those who are building the body of Christ, please consider this. God is watching. He will hold you accountable for how you build on His church. Abuse you inflict upon His people will not go unnoticed. Consider carefully this passage.

1 Corinthians 3:5-17
*Who then is Paul, and who is Apollos, but ministers through whom you believed, as the Lord gave to each one. ⁶ I planted, Apollos watered, but God gave the increase. ⁷ So then neither he who plants is anything, nor he who waters, but God who gives the increase. ⁸ Now he who plants and he who waters are one, and each one will receive his own reward according to his own labor. ⁹ For we are God's fellow workers; you are God's field, you are God's building. ¹⁰ According to the grace of God which was given to me, as a wise master builder I have laid the foundation, and another builds on it. **But let each one take heed how he builds on it.** ¹¹ For no other foundation can anyone lay than that which is laid, which is Jesus Christ. ¹² Now if anyone builds on this foundation with gold, silver, precious stones, wood, hay, straw, ¹³ each one's work will become clear; for the Day will declare it, because it will be revealed by fire; and the fire will test each one's work, of what sort it is. ¹⁴ If anyone's work which he has built on it endures, he will receive a reward. ¹⁵ If anyone's work is burned, he will suffer loss; but he himself will be saved, yet so as through fire. ¹⁶ Do you not know that you are the temple of God and that the Spirit of God dwells in you? ¹⁷ If anyone defiles the temple of God, God will destroy him. For the temple of God is holy, which temple you are.*

In context, to which temple is Paul referring here—to your body? No. He is clearly referring to the body of Christ. Whose works will be judged in this way—every believer? No. He is speaking concerning those who plant and water, the fellow workers in God's field—those who are building on the foundations of Jesus Christ. He is warning these laborers in the body of Christ to be careful how they build God's temple.

> **Ephesians 4:11-16**[37]
> *And He Himself gave some to be apostles, some prophets, some evangelists, and some pastors and teachers,* [12] *for the **equipping** of the saints for the work of ministry, for the **edifying** (building) **of the body of Christ,*** [13] *till we all come to the unity of the faith and of the knowledge of the Son of God, to a perfect man, to the measure of the stature of the fullness of Christ;* [14] *that we should no longer be children, tossed to and fro and carried about with every **wind of doctrine** (teaching), by the trickery of men, in the cunning craftiness of deceitful plotting (some "leaders" are false),* [15] *but, speaking the truth in love, may grow up in all things into Him who is the head— Christ—* [16] *from whom the whole body, joined and knit together by what every joint supplies, according to the effective working by which every part does its share, causes growth of the body for the **edifying** (building up) of itself in love.*

Those who are called in any way to build up the body of Christ are given a very stern warning in 1 Corinthians 3. Their works will be made clear as to whether they were pure and in love or deceitful and meant to oppress. In this passage, the body of Christ—those who comprise His body are referred to as the "temple of the Holy Spirit."[38] One day each of us who have the awesome responsibility to teach or to serve and love His temple, will see our works tested by fire.

---

[37] Comments in parenthesis were added by the author.

[38] In 1 Corinthians 6, it speaks of individuals as being the temple, but in this passage, taken the clear context, Paul is referring to the body of Christ as the building—the temple.

Verse 17 reveals God's attitude toward those who would defy the temple of God—the body of Christ. He will destroy that person—not in the sense of sending him to hell, but because when his works are tested, there will be little left but a pile of ashes. God's temple, the body of Christ is holy, set apart. A corrupt or abusive pastor might escape accountability while on earth, but he will give an account on that day. The spiritual authority who wronged you, if he is a true believer in Jesus, will still go to heaven, but at that moment the damage will be exposed, and the offender will at last see that his works were not acceptable before God.

Why will God do this? It is because He loves us too much to let us go into eternity thinking the wrong we did was ok. It is because He wants those who were offended to know that the damage done to them did not go unnoticed. He is both a merciful and just judge.

From the perspective of someone who at one time taught things that did not build well the body of Christ, I personally want those former works burned. If any action or teaching of mine ended up destroying God's building, please let that be burned up, too, and let only what God esteems as true building upon His temple remain.

As one who has been greatly damaged by false teaching and abusive spiritual authority, I find rest knowing that those individuals will one day stand before Jesus. It is God's job to deal with each one. It gives me comfort to know those who offended will still be with Jesus, but at some point, will be held responsible for the "wood, hay, and stubble."

For now, our responsibility is to forgive. **Forgiving does not mean what happened is "no big deal."** If false spiritual authority damaged you to the point you began to doubt the love of God for you, the offense was great. However, to be free, we must forgive. Let us therefore forgive from the heart knowing we have also been forgiven.

When anger rises again and again, turn to Jesus and forgive. When the pain spiritual abuse caused you manifests itself in some way, forgive. No, that person does not deserve your forgiveness, and in some cases doesn't even think he needs

173

your forgiveness, but God wants you to be free to love and be loved and He wants you to experience deeply His love for you.

❧ **Let go** ❧
of the anger and pain
and forgive.

"Father, thinking about the damage done in our lives by the inaccurate teachings we received as young adults, can cause us to become angry. Thinking about all of those years we wasted trying to become what You already made us, is discouraging. What misery and confusion we endured because we hadn't been taught the truth about Your grace toward us.

God, help us to accept that we must bear some responsibility for what we experienced. We had Bibles. We had brains. We chose to believe what was taught scarcely thinking to challenge it. We did not 'prove all things'. Furthermore, we ended up teaching the same errors when we began to minister. We take responsibility for what we believed and how we lived out those false beliefs.

Father, we forgive those who led us down the destructive path of self-righteousness. They, too, were deceived. Please help them and Your church to be set free from the errors that bind them—and Father, heal what was damaged by overbearing spiritual authorities. Heal the broken-hearted. Use us to share this very good news of Your love for us."

Let all bitterness and wrath and anger and clamor and slander be put away from you, along with all malice. [32] *Be kind to one another, tender-hearted, **forgiving each other**, just as God in Christ also has forgiven you.*

Ephesians 4:31-32 NASB

Continuing the Journey

In James chapter 3, we might at first focus on the damage our words can cause, and it is important for each of us to be careful about what we say, but notice in the first verse to whom this passage is primarily addressing. Then read the rest of the passage with that thought in mind.

James 3:1-18
My brethren, let not many of you become teachers, knowing that we shall receive a stricter judgment. ²*For we all stumble in many things. If anyone does not stumble in word, he is a perfect man, able also to bridle the whole body.* ³*Indeed, we put bits in horses' mouths that they may obey us, and we turn their whole body.* ⁴*Look also at ships: although they are so large and are driven by fierce winds, they are turned by a very small rudder wherever the pilot desires.* ⁵*Even so the tongue is a little member and boasts great things. See how great a forest a little fire kindles!* ⁶*And the tongue is a fire, a world of iniquity. The tongue is so set among our members that it defiles the whole body and sets on fire the course of nature; and it is set on fire by hell.* ⁷*For every kind of beast and bird, of reptile and creature of the sea, is tamed and has been tamed by mankind.* ⁸*But no man can tame the tongue. It is an unruly evil, full of deadly poison.* ⁹*With it we bless our God and Father, and with it we curse men, who have been made in the similitude of God.* ¹⁰*Out of the same mouth proceed blessing and cursing. My brethren, these things ought not to be so.* ¹¹*Does a spring send forth fresh water and bitter from the same opening?* ¹²*Can a fig tree, my brethren, bear olives, or a grapevine*

175

bear figs? Thus no spring yields both salt water and fresh.

13 Who is wise and understanding among you? **Let him show by good conduct that his works are done in the meekness of wisdom.** *14 But if you have bitter envy and self-seeking in your hearts, do not boast and lie against the truth. 15 This wisdom does not descend from above, but is earthly, sensual, demonic. 16 For where envy and self-seeking exist, confusion and every evil thing are there. 17 But the wisdom that is from above is first pure, then peaceable, gentle, willing to yield, full of mercy and good fruits, without partiality and without hypocrisy. 18 Now the fruit of righteousness is sown in peace by those who make peace.*

1. When James says teachers in the body of Christ will receive a stricter judgment before God, what does He mean? Is he speaking of eternal damnation or something else?

2. Previously, many of us thought of our words in this context as how we speak to each other, but since he is addressing teachers, to what is he more likely referring?

3. In the context of teaching, what might James mean when he says that with our tongues we bless God and curse men?

4. Consider verses 10-12 in the light of *teaching* within the body of Christ. What might this look like?

5. Consider verses 10-12 in the light of how people are *treated* in the body of Christ. What thoughts come to mind?

6. Verses 17-18 gives a guide to those who teach. How do these verses instruct the instructors?

7. As we finish Part 3: "Experiences that Hinder," are there any thoughts about your experiences in life might be in the way of confidently knowing and believing you are loved by God?

8. What role does forgiveness play in being healed of past spiritual abuse?

PART 4

Teachings that Nullify

Chapter 22

FALSE PERCEPTIONS AND ACCUSATIONS

*M*any of the reasons Christians need to *re*discover God's love for them arise because of false teachings and concepts they unwittingly embraced as truth. Jesus said we would know the truth, and the truth would set us free, but when these truths are "balanced" with untruths, the truth is negated, and we end up in bondage. These particular teachings can distance us from knowing God's love. May the Lord open our eyes so we may be free indeed from everything false.

Public Enemy Number One

From the beginning, God has been falsely mischaracterized, the goal not only being that of discrediting Him, but also of defeating the human race.

God created earth specifically for mankind. He gave them air to breathe, water to drink, food to nourish, and beauty to enjoy. He gave them companionship and meaningful tasks to complete. He only asked them not to partake of the Tree of Knowledge of Good and Evil and told them that in the day they ate of it, they would die.

The serpent came along and challenged the truth of God's word. He accused God of lying to Adam and Eve. Not only that, he impugned God's goodness by accusing Him of withholding good things from them—enlightenment and the ability to be like God (in whose image they were created).

Man had a choice, the same choice we have today: to believe God and disbelieve the enemy or to believe the enemy and disbelieve God. Do we see our God as good and doing good or do we believe the false accusation that He withholds good from us?

Propagandists

Throughout time, there have been assistants in spreading his false message contradicting the surety of God's word and His holy character. Unbelieving and ungodly persons willfully and cunningly seek to undermine His truth and spread malicious accusations against Him in literature, music, and other media. This ranges from something subtle such as a movie with a plot completely ignoring the existence of God as the main character seeks to solve some difficulty he faces, to those blatantly denying God's existence or including in the plot, motivations for not trusting Him—even reasons to loathe Him or His followers.

We watch these things in quite a numb fashion accepting that, of course, a worldly movie will express within it worldly views. We believe in God, so we don't agree with their points of view, but we watch and listen anyway, even though our beloved God is being ignored or maligned, even though our public participation might seem to endorse what is being propagated. The lies about God often go unchallenged, even in our own minds.

Don't be deceived, all of this is a deliberate attempt to secularize our mindset, the goal being, to get us to a point where we believe God is irrelevant in the affairs of our lives and make us think God is, at the very most, some force out there somewhere who is less than loving. We listen to music and watch movies and television often with our minds in neutral having become desensitized to God's character being mocked.

If you, as a believer, feel free to participate in these activities, at least do so with your mind in gear. Observe the subtle messages being sent to you about your God who gave His only begotten Son to show His love for you. Speak of these things to your children whose thinking is not as sophisticated as yours. Don't passively watch without being aware there is an attempt to malign your God and defeat you.

Personal Temptations

As we go through this life as believers in Jesus Christ, we will be tempted. At first, we think about temptation to do sinful acts, but it is much more sinister and shrewd than that. Satan's goals have not changed. He will challenge the truth of God's word, and in doing so, cast doubt upon His perfect character. "God is love," we read, and Satan's reply always begins with, "Oh, really? Well, what about..."

This is why it is of utmost importance we educate ourselves about God's love for us. If we *know* God loves us and we *believe* He loves us, we will not accept false accusations about His loving intentions toward us.

Our children know and believe we love them. They know, without a doubt, we would do anything within our abilities to help them even if it meant dying for them. Anyone could come up to them and try to convince them we don't love them, or that our intentions toward them are evil, and our kids would not believe it. They would defend our character and have nothing to do with such a person. They would not believe lies about us. Why is this? They know us. They have observed our character their entire lives and know they can trust us.

As we learn more about the goodness and love of God, and we experience His faithfulness, we become better equipped to believe in His love for us. Then, when any entity comes at us with lies about His goodness and love, we will immediately confront those lies. The enemy says, "Has God said?" and we respond, "Yes, He has."

Traditions, Superstitions, and Consensus Christianity

We expect lies to be shoveled out about our God, and we aren't surprised when those who do not know God have contrary opinions about Him, but we should also be aware there are certain "truths" circulating within the church that bring God's love into question.

Not every word spoken in a pulpit, written in a Christian book, or spoken at a religious conference is correct. We need to keep our thinking caps securely in place as we listen to teachings, songs, or while reading a book. Just because a famous Christian author, talented worship team, or renowned preacher proclaims something, doesn't mean it is true. Nor is something valid because someone posted it on social media.[39]

Perhaps you've also seen these teaching trends come and go over your lifetime. A certain teaching, not based on Scripture, is repeated so often it becomes accepted as truth. Christian song writers then put these concepts into songs. We sing them, so they must be true, right? I call this Consensus Christianity. We believe something because many teachers are teaching it and most everyone believes it. But—*is* it true? Not necessarily.

While some teachers are quite *deliberate* in what they falsely teach (their motives can only truly be known by God), the more dangerous ones are those who teach these traditions and superstitions *believing* they are correct.

While God will hold false teachers accountable, each believer is individually responsible to listen and evaluate what he hears. When something is taught that casts doubt on God's goodness and the veracity of His promises to us, we need to take the time to refute that teaching because, you see, the *motivation* behind a false teaching isn't what damages us—it's the *teaching* itself. One teacher might be trying to manipulate you and another sincerely trying to help you, but if either one feeds you poison, you will get sick. That's why **we** must take

---

[39] These topics are discussed in much more detail in <u>Overcoming the Overwhelming</u>.

responsibility to, "Prove all things and hold fast to that which is good," (1 Th. 5:21).

There are many Christians whose lives are a clear reflection of God's love. We can see God's love manifested in how they speak, how they interact with others, in what they teach about God, and even in how they go through difficulties. Perhaps you were blessed with parents who not only taught you about God's love, but who showed you His love by how they treated you.

Perhaps your parents fell short in this area, but you married someone whose life and love for you clearly portrays the love of God. Even if your spouse is not a perfect example, perhaps you know God's love via your love for your own children and perhaps by their love for you.

It is wonderful to love and to be loved, but we must always keep in mind what my mother repeatedly taught me, "People will fail you, Cathy, but Jesus never will. Keep your eyes on Jesus." Yes, there might be many people who radiate the love of God, but even if *they* fail you, this is not a reflection on our God. His love for you, unlike human love, is constant and infallible. His love never fails.

"Father, we choose to believe You are good and You love us. We reject every voice that rises in accusation against You. We live in a world that is so corrupt, one that scoffs at the thought of Your existence and ridicules those who believe in You. Yet You still reach out to us in love. Father, we receive Your love and believe in Your goodness."

When the kindness and the love of God our Savior toward man appeared, ⁵ not by works of righteousness which we have done, but according to His mercy He saved us, through the washing of regeneration and renewing of the Holy Spirit, ⁶ whom He poured out on us abundantly through Jesus Christ our Savior, ⁷ that having been justified by His grace we should become heirs according to the hope of eternal life.

Titus 3:4-7

Continuing the Journey

1. What would you say are the world's perceptions of God, or what were your perceptions before you knew Him personally?

2. When I was a child, television shows and some movies openly mentioned God in a favorable way. In addition, morality was an admired trait. Most shows had some moral to the story. If you are old enough to have observed the progression away from God and morality in our media, share some of what you've seen.

3. Have you ever gone through a difficult situation in which you felt God's love for you was put in question? How did you deal with the false accusations against Him?

4. Can you think of some traditions, superstitions, or false teachings that robbed you from knowing and believing God's love for you personally?

5. *Without naming names*, has a Christian whom you loved and admired let you down in some way? Did this affect your perception of God's love for you?

6. How does keeping our eyes on Jesus help us when others fail us?

7. As you rediscover God's great love for you, He will likely unravel false thoughts in your heart you cannot right now identify. When you realize He is showing you something, take the time to discover the truth in each and every situation and give Him time to heal any damage done.

Chapter 23

HORROR INSTEAD OF HOPE

Our Supremely Happy, Joyful, and Confident Anticipation

Titus 2:11-14

For the grace of God that brings salvation has appeared to all men, 12 teaching us that, denying ungodliness and worldly lusts, we should live soberly, righteously, and godly in the present age, 13 looking for the blessed hope and glorious appearing of our great God and Savior Jesus Christ, 14 who gave Himself for us, that He might redeem us from every lawless deed and purify for Himself His own special people, zealous for good works.

The glorious appearing of our great God and Savior Jesus Christ is something for which we are *looking*. It is our "blessed hope." The word "hope" in the Greek translates, "joyful and confident expectation of eternal salvation,"[40] "Blessed" means, "supremely blessed, happy." Our blessed hope is thus our supremely happy, joyful, and confident anticipation of our eternal salvation. Yes, we *have* eternal life right now (1 Jn.

---

[40] Thayer

5:13), but we also look forward to a time when we shall forever be with our beloved Jesus.

> **1 Thessalonians 4:13-18**
> *But I do not want you to be ignorant, brethren, concerning those who have fallen asleep, lest you sorrow as others who have no hope. [14] For if we believe that Jesus died and rose again, even so God will bring with Him those who sleep in Jesus. [15] For this we say to you by the word of the Lord, that* **we who are alive and remain until the coming of the Lord will by no means precede those who are asleep.** *[16] For the Lord Himself will descend from heaven with a shout, with the voice of an archangel, and with the trumpet of God. And the dead in Christ will rise first. [17]* **Then we who are alive and remain shall be caught up together with them in the clouds to meet the Lord in the air. And thus we shall always be with the Lord.** *[18] Therefore comfort one another with these words.*

There is no historical record of the dead in Christ rising and millions of Christians being snatched off the earth, so this glorious day is still in the future which is precisely why we look forward to it.

> **1 John 3:2-3**
> *Beloved, now we are children of God; and it has not yet been revealed what we shall be, but we know that when He is revealed, we shall be like Him, for we shall see Him as He is. [3] And everyone who has this hope in Him purifies himself, just as He is pure.*

Think about that; the joyful anticipation of His return is *in* us, and we are actually purified by this hope. His coming was never meant to be a frightening event for God's children; instead it is our happy hope and source of comfort. Those who died in Jesus will rise again, and those of us who are still alive when this happens will join them in the air. Imagine the reunion when many of us see dear friends, parents, grandparents, cousins, and siblings, whose losses we mourned and whose lives we have missed, rising together to meet Jesus in the air!

> *When we all get to heaven,*
> *What a day of rejoicing that will be!*
> *When we all see Jesus,*
> *We'll sing and shout the victory![41]*

Get Ready

Yet for far too many believers, the supremely happy, joyful, and confident anticipation of His return has been morphed into a dreadful, fearful, and questionable event. Scriptures are taken out of context and some of them completely ignored in an effort to cast doubt upon our sure redemption, often in a misguided effort to manipulate us into not sinning. We are told to "be ready" because He could come at any moment, and the clear implication is that if we "have sin in our lives" at His appearing, we will be left behind. This is simply not true. Christians will not be left behind because of sin because, dearly loved of God, He is not holding our sins against us.

> ### Romans 4:5-8
> *But to him who does not work but believes on Him who justifies the ungodly, his faith is accounted for righteousness, [6] just as David also describes the blessedness of the man to whom God imputes righteousness apart from works: [7] "Blessed are those whose lawless deeds are forgiven, And whose sins are covered;*

---

[41] Emily D. Wilson, *pub.* 1898, © *Public Domain; and of course, there is nothing stopping us from singing and shouting the victory now!*

> *⁸ Blessed is the man to whom the Lord <u>shall not impute sin</u>.”*

You and I are the blessed ones of whom David speaks. God is not keeping record of our sins. We are completely and forevermore forgiven (Heb. 10).

Unholy Coercions

Here is another teaching prevalent among Christians, that even if someone isn't "sinning," the mere fact someone might not be "spiritual" *enough*, "dedicated" *enough*, "diligent" *enough*, close *enough*, and faithful *enough* would be causes for missing out on the Rapture and being forced to endure the great Tribulation. Others see the Tribulation as a means by which God will purify the church of its sinfulness (as if the blood of Jesus wasn't enough).

At some point, one has to wonder if any Christian would be worthy *enough* to meet the Lord in the air. Picture a few hundred rising from their graves and maybe a thousand worldwide joining them in the air.

Some of you know I am not exaggerating because the coming of Jesus has been hung over your head like an anvil ready to fall any moment. You may have lived with a dread of God all your life. "Conform or else!" No wonder so many people don't want anything to do with "Christianity" and many leave the church. My brothers and sisters, we need never fear our blessed hope.

> ### 1 John 4:17-18 NASB
> *By this, love is perfected with us, so that we may have **confidence in the day of judgment**; because as He is, so also are we in this world. ¹⁸ **There is no fear in love; but perfect love casts out fear**, because fear involves punishment, and the one who fears is not perfected in love.*

Blessed Assurance

> *1 John 5:13 AMP*
> *These things I have written to you who believe in the name of the Son of God [which represents all that Jesus Christ is and does], so that you will know [with settled and absolute knowledge] that you [already] have eternal life.*

Our hope is a supremely happy joyful anticipation for a reason—because it is *assured*. It is a settled and absolute fact we already have eternal life. This is what Jesus died to give all of those who believe in Him—everlasting life. We can't earn it nor need we maintain it.

> *John 3:16*
> *For God so loved the world, that He gave His only begotten Son, that whoever BELIEVES in him shall* **not** *perish, but have* **everlasting** *life.*
> *John 3:18 AMP*
> *Whoever BELIEVES and has decided to trust in Him [as personal Savior and Lord] is* **not** **judged** *[for this one, there is no judgment, no rejection, no condemnation.]*

For those who believe, there is no longer a fear of condemnation for we are free from the law. When we were His *enemies*, Jesus died for us. Now that we are reconciled to God as beloved children, we are saved by His life.

> *Romans 8:1 AMP*
> *Therefore there is now no condemnation [no guilty verdict, no punishment] for those who are in Christ Jesus.*
> *Romans 5:9-10*
> ***Much more then, having now been justified by His blood, we shall be saved from wrath through Him.*** *[10] For if when we were enemies*

> we were reconciled to God through the
> death of His Son, **much more, having been
> reconciled, we shall be saved by His life.**

A Thief in the Night

The idea that Jesus will come as a thief in the night is also used to scare the hope out of us and fill us with fear, but we must see this passage in its context. I'm sure as you read it, you will see we need not fear His coming.

> *1 Thessalonians 5:1-11*
> *But concerning the times and the seasons,
> brethren, you have no need that I should write
> to you.* ² *For you yourselves know perfectly that
> the day of the Lord so comes as a thief in the
> night.* ³ *For when they say, "Peace and safety!"
> then sudden destruction comes upon them, as
> labor pains upon a pregnant woman. And they
> shall not escape.* ⁴ ***But you, brethren***, *are not in
> darkness, so that this Day should overtake you
> as a thief.* ⁵ *You are all sons of light and sons of
> the day. We are not of the night nor of darkness.*
> ⁶ *Therefore let us not sleep, as others do, but
> let us watch and be sober.* ⁷ *For those who
> sleep, sleep at night, and those who get drunk
> are drunk at night.* ⁸ *But let us who are of the
> day be sober, putting on the breastplate of faith
> and love, and as a helmet the **hope** of salvation.*
> ⁹ ***For God did not appoint us to wrath, but
> to obtain salvation through our Lord Jesus
> Christ,*** ¹⁰ ***who died for us, that whether we
> wake or sleep, we should live together with
> Him.*** ¹¹ *Therefore **comfort** each other and edify
> one another, just as you also are doing.*

His coming will not be like a thief in the night for us. Our houses are ready for God abides in us. We are looking for His coming as our blessed hope. We aren't appointed to wrath. We are appointed to obtain deliverance when He appears. Glory to God!

Eternal Security

This topic has been studied, discussed, and debated throughout the centuries. The extremes range from the idea any believer could end up in hell based on sin in his life because God is holy, and no unholy person will be in heaven, to the notion that it is impossible for anyone who was born again to be lost, even if that person renounces Christ.

The truth, in my humble evaluation, is that sin has been dealt with thoroughly. All our sins were forgiven at the cross. No believer, however imperfect, will be lost due to sin. (Sigh of relief!) The determining factor as to whether someone will be saved is **faith** in Jesus. Those who believe in Him WILL NOT PERISH but have EVERLASTING life. Those who do not believe in Him, Jesus said, will be condemned.

> ### John 3:17-19
> *"For God did not send His Son into the world to condemn the world, but that the world through Him might be saved. [18] He who believes in Him is not condemned; but **he who does not believe is condemned already**, because he has not believed in the name of the only begotten Son of God. [19] And this is the condemnation, that the light has come into the world, and men loved darkness rather than light, because their deeds were evil."*

A Reason to Rest

There are many things the death and resurrection of Jesus provides, and one of them is that those who believe in Him will not come into judgment. Do you believe in Him? Then you are and will be saved on that day. Once this is settled in your mind, instead of working to obtain or maintain what you have already been given, you may **live** freely with full confidence and joyful anticipation during this life. When we face persecutions or difficulties, we don't need to worry. Not only can we rest knowing these things cannot separate us from His love, we can look forward to a day when we will be completely free.

> **Romans 8:18-23**
> *For I consider that the sufferings of this present time are not worthy to be compared with the glory which shall be revealed in us. ¹⁹ For the earnest expectation of the creation eagerly waits for the revealing of the sons of God. ²⁰ For the creation was subjected to futility, not willingly, but because of Him who subjected it in hope; ²¹ because the creation itself also will be delivered from the bondage of corruption into the glorious liberty of the children of God. ²² For we know that the whole creation groans and labors with birth pangs together until now. ²³ Not only that, but we also who have the firstfruits of the Spirit, even we ourselves groan within ourselves, eagerly waiting for the adoption, the redemption of our body.*

We tend to get caught up in the day to day experience, but we need to remind ourselves and each other that this life we live on earth is not "it." We have a reason to hope—to happily and joyfully look forward to His appearing when these mortal bodies shall become immortal.

> **1 Corinthians 15:51-58**
> *Behold, I tell you a mystery: We shall not all sleep, but we shall all be changed— ⁵² in a moment, in the twinkling of an eye, at the last trumpet. For the trumpet will sound, and the dead will be raised incorruptible, and we shall be changed. ⁵³ **For this corruptible must put***

on incorruption, and this mortal must put on immortality. *[54] So when this corruptible has put on incorruption, and this mortal has put on immortality, then shall be brought to pass the saying that is written: "Death is swallowed up in victory.*
[55] "O Death, where is your sting?
O Hades, where is your victory?
[56] The sting of death is sin, and the strength of sin is the law. [57] But thanks be to God, who gives us the victory through our Lord Jesus Christ.
[58] Therefore, my beloved brethren, be steadfast, immovable, always abounding in the work of the Lord, knowing that your labor is not in vain in the Lord.

We tend to think of His coming as an exhilarating event, but can you envision the love that will encircle us at the moment when the God who sent His Son out of love to save us from our sin and who has loved us every day since, sends Jesus again to gather His own dearly beloved children from the four corners of the earth to save us from the wrath which is to come? I can picture the joy on each face, not only ours, but His! The love that sent Him to demonstrate His love to us will one day gather us together, and we will be caught up to Him by His love and live with Him forever.

"Jesus, we believe You will come again for Your own—for all of us who believe in You, even those whose lives are not perfect. How we look forward to being caught up together with You in the air, to putting on immortality and incorruption, and to seeing You face to face.

When we consider this coming rapture, our hearts fill with delight and no longer with fear because we now know You saved us by grace through faith.

"Help us to remember Your coming when life becomes overwhelming—when it looks like the walls are crashing in on us.

Help us to focus on Your sure return. Knowing You will return for the ones You love brings such comfort and joy. Help us to remember the glory that will be revealed in us on that day."

> *O, I want to see Him*
> *Look upon His face,*
> *There to sing forever*
> *Of His saving grace.*
> *On the streets of Glory*
> *Let me lift my voice,*
> *Cares all past,*
> *Home at last*
> *Ever to rejoice.*[42]

Continuing the Journey

1. Was there a time in your Christian life you feared the coming of the Lord? If so, why do you think this was so?

2. Did you ever come home to an empty house and think maybe the Lord returned and you were left behind?

3. Was His coming ever used to motivate/manipulate you into certain modes of behavior as a Christian?

4. His return is called our blessed hope. Explain your response to His return being our "supremely happy, joyful, confident anticipation."

5. What images are in your mind about how this event will take place?

---

[42] Rufus Henry Cornelius, 1916, Public Domain

6. How can the hope of His return to gather His own both purify and comfort us?

7. On a little table next to my desk, there is a small stone that reads, "hope." I often look at this to remind myself of the glorious truth of His return. Can you think of ways you might remind yourself of your blessed hope?

Chapter 24

CONDITIONAL LOVE

*P*robably the most damaging teachings today spring forth from the idea that God's love is conditional. There are many teachings along this line, but we all understand if someone tells us he will love us based on certain conditions, this is conditional, flimsy love. It is a love that is only as strong as our behavior merits and thus destined for nothing but insecurity.

Old Covenant Thinking

The most influential reason many of us develop the idea of God's love as being conditional is the church is still unaware we are not under any part of the law. Even if a church does state clearly that we are not under any part of the law including the Ten Commandments, there can still exist many law-based beliefs. These beliefs can tarnish our perception of God's love for us.

Under the law, the Jews were blessed IF they obeyed the law BUT if they didn't, they would be cursed. We might think this is conditional love, but actually, the *blessings and curses* were conditional, not God's love. God's love for Israel, even under the law system, was not based on their behavior.

> **Jeremiah 31:3**
> *"I have loved you with an everlasting love;*

I have drawn you with unfailing kindness."
Matthew 23:27
*"Jerusalem, Jerusalem, you who kill the prophets
and stone those sent to you, how often I have
longed to gather your children together, as a
hen gathers her chicks under her wings, and
you were not willing."*

If we are not careful, we can begin to think that when bless-ings come our way it is because God loves us, and when we experience hard times, it is because God is withholding His love so He can teach or punish us. If we maintain a law mindset and we fall short of living up to whatever standard has been set before us (even the laws we set for ourselves), we can *feel* unworthy of His love. We can go to bed or wake up feeling we are letting God down—with condemnation and shame following us as a perpetual shadow, perhaps living in a constant state of doom being certain that any day now, God is going to punish us.

Or if we think we *do* merit God's blessings and love because we are keeping the standards we believe He requires, we can become offended and shocked when difficulties come our way. With a fist in the air we might cry, "God, I've done everything you've asked me to do, why is this happening to me?

The "Real" World

From the cradle to the grave in this life we are recom-pensed for being good and penalized when we aren't. As chil-dren, we are often rewarded for good behavior or end up in timeout or get a spanking when we misbehave. In education, we study hard, put lots of work into projects or reports, and as a result, get good grades. **Subtly, we can start to think our relationship with God is bettered by our productivity.**

Similarly, in most careers there are rewards for a job well-done, but we will likely lose our jobs if we are negligent. These are considered normal consequences and need not be seen as having anything to do with God. Someone who believes in

God and someone who doesn't, will both be rewarded for good work and face the consequences of laziness. Now, our boss might like us based on many factors, but usually an excellent worker with a positive attitude will progress on the job. Your employer might be a relative or a best friend, but even with this advantage, you will likely lose your job if your performance is substandard.

Amazingly, God is not like this. He will not disown you for not being perfect. He will continue to work in your life to bring you to where He wants you to be. In fact, God might even bless you when you do not "deserve" it in the least.

Relationships

The relationships we experience with other human beings, for better or worse, are considerably conditional. I'm not saying it should be this way, only that it often is.

Two people may be the best of friends in the world but let one of them begin to treat the other with unkindness, that relationship will be damaged and might even fade away.

A man and woman may promise to love "for better, for worse; in sickness and in health, for richer or poorer, to love and to cherish as long as we both shall live," but many spouses do not keep their vows and soon hit the road seeking greener pastures.

When the people who should love us unconditionally don't, we can begin to conclude we are not worthy of love, not even God's.

However, even if the whole world forsakes us,
❧ God will still love us. ❦

The Pouting God

God's love cannot be compared to human love because human love is extremely limited. Yet we do often attribute to God the sentiments of man in an effort to understand Him—a practice we need to employ sparingly. Yes, God is our Father, and yes, there are a few fathers who reflect the love of God, but sadly, many parents fall woefully short of demonstrating God's love. Let's take another look at these verses to illustrate this point.

> **Romans 5:7-8**
> *For scarcely for a righteous man will one die; yet perhaps for a good man someone would even dare to die.* [8] ***But God** **demonstrates** **His own love toward us, in that while we were still sinners, Christ died for us.***

Notice that the goodness and love of man is being *contrasted* to God's love. It is unlikely someone would die even for a righteous person, even though perhaps for a good person, someone might possibly die. BUT (and this is a good "but"), God's love isn't like that. His love is so extreme, He died for those who were neither righteous nor good. This is the kind of love He holds out for us to see. He wants us to know that no matter how awful we might think we are or how horrible we might think someone else is, He died for all because *He* loves us all.

When we understand God's love is far superior to ours and that it is wiser to *contrast* human love to God's rather than *compare* it, we are better able to rejoice that God does not respond to us with the impatience and unkindness humankind often does.

God doesn't pout when He doesn't get His way in our lives. Instead, He continues to work in us "both to will and to do of His good pleasure," (Phil. 2:13). He isn't disappointed with us when we make a choice in life that isn't the best. Rather, He begins to work all things together for our good, even our mistakes (Rom. 8:28).

He doesn't put us on a shelf when our usefulness to His kingdom seems to wane. His love doesn't give up on us when we aren't the successes others think we should be. We may feel washed out. Those who look on our lives may do so with pity or disappointment, but God sees our hearts. When we are downcast, He comforts us, encourages us, prunes us, and gives us the rest we need so we may once again bear fruit (Jn. 15:2).

Finally, God's love is not vindictive. You may feel like "the powers that be" are doing all they can to thwart your efforts and punish you, but I guarantee you, this is not your God. He is not condemning you nor seeking to harm you. He is working against all such activity so you may know His kindness and love for you.

God's Discipline

Some will say, "Doesn't God discipline His children?" Yes, He does, but not in the way earthly parents do. First, God's discipline will never at any time include a physical punishment. You will not perceive with your eyes the discipline of God, but you will surely begin to recognize it in your heart.

Godly discipline is when God shows you something you are **believing** or something you are **doing** is wrong. It IS painful as we see in the passage below, but not physically painful.

Many times, deep in my heart, God has corrected what I believe. It is not enjoyable to discover a long-held belief is incorrect. For example, most of my life I believed if I sinned, I had to confess my sins *in order to be* forgiven. I treasured that "truth" because it had been my practice for so many years. It was something "I" could do about getting my sins forgiven even though I knew in my heart only His blood could deal with sin.

When I realized I was wrong, completely wrong, it was almost shocking to me. I was flabbergasted I was still holding on to a tradition I'd been taught and that it was due to me not seeing a passage of Scripture for what it was really saying (1 Jn. 1). I almost felt embarrassed. Yet the revelation set me freer than I'd ever been. God corrected my belief. Initially, it was painful to admit I'd been wrong, but accepting the correction brought great freedom and joy into my Christian walk.

Hebrews 12:9-11
Furthermore, we have had human fathers who

202

> **corrected** *us, and we paid them respect. Shall we not much more readily be in subjection to the Father of spirits and live?* *¹⁰ For they indeed for a few days chastened us as seemed best to them, but He for our profit, that we may be partakers of His holiness.* *¹¹ Now no chastening seems to be joyful for the present, but painful; nevertheless, afterward it yields the peaceable fruit of righteousness to those who have been trained by it.*

The original context of this passage had to do with the author's efforts to correct the behavior and beliefs of the Hebrews. They were clinging to the law instead of whole-heartedly embracing Jesus.

It's important to notice "chastening" is being compared to correction. It isn't referring to being beaten. We need to notice that He is *contrasting not comparing* His correction with our earthly fathers. They chastened us as seemed best to *them*, but God corrects us for *our* profit! Though correction is not enjoyable while it's happening; yes indeed, sometimes it is even painful, it yields the peaceable fruit of righteousness when we are trained by it.

This also is true when God points out a certain behavior or attitudes that are not correct. We may feel a moment of uncomfortableness, especially when our actions were public and will likely involve needing to apologize or making restitution, but we also sense His forgiveness and grace through it all with the added benefit of being set free from the thing that had us bound.

Some believers confuse guilt and shame with being corrected by God, but there is an enormous difference. The best way to differentiate between them is this: when we are being shamed or feel guilty, it is because we see a fault, but there is no way to resolve the issue. So, our minds just go in circles with no answer. When God corrects us, there is always a solution followed by the ability to change and peace. The enemy wants to keep us down and defeated by constant accusations.

God wants to set us free by correcting our course. God does not need to send troubles into our lives to bring about good.

He is a far superior communicator than that.

We are led by His Spirit and taught by His grace (Rom. 8:14, Ti. 2:11-14). We are His sheep. We hear and know His voice (Jn. 10:27-30). Most importantly, He speaks directly to us and not through human mediators. He is perfectly capable of speaking directly to us, through Scripture, by His Spirit, and by His grace.

There are no prerequisites to be loved by God, for He loved us without condition when He gave His Son on the cross for us when we were ungodly. He bled for us when we were His enemies. How much more will His love toward His dearly beloved children be unconditional.

"Jesus, thank-You for Your unconditional love and for being who You say You are. Lord, we welcome Your discipline and correction in our lives. We are not afraid of Your instruction. This is because You will do us no harm. We are Your children. If there is something we are believing that is not correct, You will teach us by Your grace. If we are heading down a wrong path, Your Spirit will lead us. If our behavior in any way does not bring You praise, thank-You for correcting us. Even though discipline is not joyous and sometimes difficult, we joyfully anticipate the peace You intend to bring into our lives as a result of it. Thank-You for being the most superior communicator that exists and that You don't need to bring trouble into our lives to get through to us. You are perfectly capable of speaking to us. Thank-You, Father that Your love for us is not comparable to human love. You loved us when we were trying to deny You. You patiently lead us to You. We trust that now that we are your children, You are doing the same—except now, You live inside of us, and made us new creations, capable of hearing Your voice. Thank-You for your unconditional love for us."

For if when we were enemies
we were reconciled to God
through the death of His Son,
MUCH MORE, having been reconciled,
we shall be saved by His life.

Romans 5:10

Continuing the Journey

1. How can these areas or topics ill-inform us about God's love?
   - Old Covenant thinking
   - The "real" world
   - Imperfect human relationships

2. Why is it better to **contrast** God's love with human love rather than to compare it?

3. Discuss some of the human attributes often attributed to God and discuss how these can negatively affect our perspective of God's love for us.

4. How does God discipline/correct us? In what ways is this different or similar to the way human fathers correct us?

Chapter 25

NEVER COMPLETE

---

*A*part from Christ (which we are not, nor shall we ever be), we are merely living beings roaming the earth seeking to know our worth. Any validation of our value we might generate by ourselves will be based on the self-righteousness of works because, in this world, one's value is assessed by what one accomplishes.

In Christ our righteousness is by faith in Him *apart* from works.

> **Titus 3:5**
> *Not by works of righteousness which we have done, but according to His mercy He saved us.*
> **Ephesians 2:8-9**
> *For by grace you have been saved through faith, and that not of yourselves; it is the gift of God, [9] not of works, lest anyone should boast.*

Most Christian teachers and preachers would agree that when we are born again, we are forgiven of all our past wrongs and are made new creations by grace through faith—that we cannot earn salvation. However, it is very commonly taught that after being saved by grace through faith (and not works), that it is now our task to live by law through works. No, it will not likely be stated this way, but the idea will always be that Jesus got the ball rolling, but now it's up to us to keep it moving.

This is the very lie that sends so many Christians down the meaningless path of self-improvement and eventual dissatisfaction leading to misery—sometimes worse than the life they knew before Jesus. Blood-bought believers who are born knowing they are right with God and who are initially assured of His love for them, can grow dull in their awareness of these gifts because someone is teaching them they need to become increasingly more holy and more righteous. Subtly, the idea creeps in we will never be good enough for God to truly love us. We might *say* we know God loves us, but deep inside, we see no *reason* why He would.

If this is you, it is important you be confident of these two statements concerning who you are before God. 1) You are already holy. 2) You are already righteous. The proof of these two important facts is simple to verify, so simple that we still marvel that for so long we didn't see it, and that for so many years we suffered because we didn't have a clue about what Jesus accomplished when he died and rose again.

You Are Holy

Below is a key passage to help us understand we are already permanently holy before God based on what *Jesus* did for us. Just in case you aren't aware, the word "sanctify" means "to make holy."

Another interesting fact about these synonyms is that it is where we get the word "saint." "Saint" can be translated "holy one" or "sanctified one." (Comments have been placed within this passage in brackets and boldface so you can more clearly understand this important point—you are right now holy.)

Hebrews 10:8-14 NASB [with commentary]
*After saying above, "SACRIFICES AND OFFERINGS AND WHOLE BURNT OFFERINGS AND sacrifices FOR SIN YOU HAVE NOT DESIRED, NOR HAVE YOU TAKEN PLEASURE in them" (which are offered according to the Law), ⁹ then He said, "BEHOLD, I HAVE COME TO DO YOUR WILL." He takes away the first [**the***

Old Covenant] *in order to establish the second* **[the New Covenant].** *¹⁰ By this will* **[God's will for Christ to die for us]** *we <u>have been sanctified</u>* **[notice the past tense]** *through the offering of the body of Jesus Christ <u>once for all</u>.* **[How was it that we were sanctified/made holy? It was through Christ's death.] [Does this process of being made holy need to be repeated? No. It was "once for all."]**

¹¹ Every priest stands daily ministering and offering time after time the same sacrifices, which can never take away sins; **[Notice here that being made holy has to do with having our sins taken away.]** *¹² but He, having <u>offered one sacrifice for sins for all time</u>* **[forgiveness of sins has already happened; it doesn't need to be repeated as under the Old Covenant]**, SAT DOWN AT THE RIGHT HAND OF GOD, *¹³ waiting from that time onward* UNTIL HIS ENEMIES BE MADE A FOOTSTOOL FOR HIS FEET. *¹⁴ For by <u>one</u> offering* **[by HIS ONE offering—not ours)** *He has* **[HE has—not we]** *perfected for all time* **[perfected here is referring to our forgiveness—we are completely forgiven for <u>all</u> time]** *those who are sanctified* **[Christians ARE sanctified/ made holy—for all time].**

You already ARE holy. What do you think you could do to make yourself **more** holy? What can we do that is more powerful than His death? Ours? God forbid! We are holy because He has made us holy through His one-time sacrifice. That is precisely why Paul wrote that we are saved by grace through faith and "not of works." Try saying this with confidence.

I am holy before God.
❧ I am a saint of God. ❧

If you find it difficult to say you are a holy saint of God, you are not alone. Saying such things to us sounds like boasting. However, when we truly understand that there is nothing we can do to make ourselves holy, and that our holiness is a gift by grace through faith, we discover that instead of thinking these statements as boasting in ourselves, we begin to see them as boasting in our God. Gratitude and rest follow.

You Are Righteous

It is also important we understand we are already righteous. This means we are justified before God. We are not only right before God by faith, we are the very righteousness **of God** (2 Cor. 5:21). There is nothing we can do to make ourselves more righteous. It is because we ARE righteous/justified that we live righteously—NOT that we are righteous BECAUSE we live righteously. Righteousness is by faith in Jesus, not by works. Can you say this with confidence?

❧ I am the righteousness of God in Christ Jesus. ❧

Can you see the insanity of going to church each Sunday and instead of it being affirmed we are both holy and righteous, we are rebuked because we are not holy or righteous *enough*? In essence, what Jesus has done for us is being negated.

"Get right with God," the poor youth group students are told several times a year. Have they ever heard that because they believe in Jesus they ARE right with Him? Can you imagine the shock on some of their faces if they heard this good news? Consider the revival such teaching would ignite!

> ### *Romans 5:1-2*
> *Therefore, having **been** justified by <u>faith</u>, we have peace with God through our Lord Jesus Christ, ² through whom also we have access by faith into this grace in which we stand, and rejoice in hope of the glory of God.*

There is endless power and rest in knowing we need not improve on what He has done. Yes, we will grow. We will mature. We will learn. We will be transformed. All of these things, however, will be His doing.

> **Colossians 2:6-10**
> **As** *you therefore have received Christ Jesus the Lord,* **so walk in Him**, *⁷ rooted and built up and established in the* **faith**, *as you have been taught, abounding in* **it** *with thanksgiving. ⁸ Beware lest anyone cheat you through philosophy and empty deceit, according to the tradition of men, according to the basic principles of the world, and not according to Christ. ⁹ For in* **Him** *dwells* **all** *the fullness of the Godhead bodily; ¹⁰ and* **you are complete in Him**, *who is the head of all principality and power.*

We received Jesus by grace through faith, and that is how we walk in Him. Amazingly, we are complete (replete) in Him. We don't need to strive to **be holy and righteous *enough*** so that He will love us or love us more. He loved us when we were dead sinners. How much more does He love us now that we are His holy and righteous children.

"Father, thank-You that You made us complete in You and that by Your sacrifice You perfected us forever. Today, we let go of our own efforts to be right with You and turn to You to do in us what You desire. By faith, we are holy and righteous before You. We are justified. We are your saints. We are sanctified. Help us to walk in the same manner in which we were saved—by grace through faith. Thank-You for this great love that reached out to us when we were Your enemies and made us Your friends."

I have been crucified with Christ; it is no longer I who live,
but Christ lives in me
and the life which I now live in the flesh
I live by faith in the Son of God
<u>who loved me</u>
and gave Himself for me.
[21] *I do not set aside the grace of God*
for if righteousness comes through the law,
then Christ died in vain."

Galatians 2:20-21

Continuing the Journey

1. What correlations do you see between thinking we need to make ourselves good enough and not being certain of God's love for us?

2. How will knowing we are already holy and righteous before God positively affect our relationship with Him?

Chapter 26

NEVER ENOUGH

Without any doubt, one of the most devastating teachings that separated us from being convinced of God's love for us was the concept there was always something "more" that needed to be done to please God.

Pleasing God was the most important thing in my life. For that reason, I was determined that every word, deed, and even every thought of mine would honor Him. Yet all my efforts only brought me misery because that golden carrot of being pleasing to God was always ten steps ahead of me. This is how I described my experience in my second book.

> Diligently seeking to be close to Him and seeking to love Him with all of my heart, my soul, and my strength, yet not being totally assured of how deeply He loved me brought emptiness and misery. As I was heading down a prescribed road to righteousness, I was convinced I was correct in my pursuits. "I" would please God. "I" would live a holy life. "I" would practice my spiritual disciplines. "I" would love God with all of my being. "I" would be a good wife and mother. "I" would make sure that every thought and word and deed of mine was honest and pure. "I" would give. "I" would love others as Christ loved me. "I" would overcome the overwhelming areas of my life.
>
> Please understand this, I didn't see this as

self-righteousness, but as my desire to please God and be holy—to be diligent and faithful.

*In my zealous pursuit of holiness, I lost sight of the fact that by "His" blood, once and for all, "He" made me holy. "He" brought me close. "He" forgave all of my sins. By "His" grace through faith, "He" made me "His" righteousness. By "His" wounds I was healed. "He" was my wisdom. By "His" doing I was in Christ. "He" gave me an anointing. "He" brought about revival. "He" loved me, yes, me personally, and "He" loved me without condition. All these things that "He" did, I was trying to **better**.*

No wonder God seemed far away! Of course my perception of His love for me, the love I knew the first day I believed in Him, was diminished. Religious laws and goals mixed in with societal expectations had snuffed out nearly every trace of the life that was in me. Seeking my own righteousness through my own efforts, caused me to be "estranged from Christ" even though I was not involved in sin and desired so greatly to please Him and glorify His name.

Anyone who seeks to be justified by law will fall from His grace.
❧ It is automatic. ❦
God loves us too much to allow us to feel comfortable continuing down the dead road of self-effort.

More rational souls detected this error sooner and found a different place of fellowship, but "I" would be one of the diligent ones who kept on doing "more."

When coming to my lowest point in my Christian walk— when God seemed very far away, and His love was barely perceivable, I was actually asking God to show me what *else* He wanted me **to do**—anything so I could once again know

His love for me. Patiently, He waited for me to return to Him again by grace through faith.

Upon returning to Him for grace, the distance and lack of love and misery instantly disappeared. It all seemed too good to be true at first, but the love and awareness of His presence that was with me could not be denied. It would take many years for God to untangle all the rules and regulations tied across my heart, but God patiently and faithfully untied each one, and each time, His life would flow in that area of my life, and His love was more dearly perceived.

"Father, for so many years, so many of us worked so hard to be the best Christians we could be. We tried to do everything we believed You wanted us to do. We sought to please You with every word and deed because we so deeply loved You. Yet many of us became estranged from your power because, without knowing it, we were seeking to be right before You based on what "we" did for You—by following all the disciplines we were told would bring us closer. We see now, we were wrong. Your love for us is not based on us following spiritual laws or being the perfect Christians. We can do nothing to merit Your love which you give by Your grace. You love us. Period. You were pleased with us the day we turned to you in faith, and faith is how we please you now. Please help us to see that believing in You is enough, and that from this basic loving relationship, everything You plan for our lives will flow. All we think and do will be a result of our right-standing with You."

*You have become estranged from Christ,
you who attempt to be justified by law; you
have fallen from grace. ⁵ For we through
the Spirit eagerly wait for the hope of
righteouness by faith. ⁶ For in Christ Jesus
neither circumcision nor uncircumcision avails
anything **but faith working through love.***

Galatians 5:4-6

Continuing the Journey

1. Read the following passage. Who is doing the work here? Why is this important to notice?

    > **Jeremiah 31:31-34**
    > *"Behold, the days are coming, says the L*ORD*, when I will make a new covenant with the house of Israel and with the house of Judah—* ³² *not according to the covenant that I made with their fathers in the day that I took them by the hand to lead them out of the land of Egypt, My covenant which they broke, though I was a husband to them, says the L*ORD*.* ³³ *But this is the covenant that I will make with the house of Israel after those days, says the L*ORD*: I will put My law in their minds, and write it on their hearts; and I will be their God, and they shall be My people.* ³⁴ *No more shall every man teach his neighbor, and every man his brother, saying, 'Know the L*ORD*,' for they all shall know Me, from the least of them to the greatest of them, says the L*ORD*. For I will forgive their iniquity, and their sin I will remember no more."*

2. On my office desk, I have a small framed saying my daughter made for me. It reads, "Let all that you do today be enough." Have you ever felt trapped feeling you can never do enough? If you have escaped this trap, share how this came about. Do you ever catch yourself falling back into that way of thinking?

Chapter 27

GOD'S FAVORITES

---

*T*he conclusions we came to about God having favorites and loving some of His children more than others were gradually acquired beliefs. One of the teachings that led us to such an inaccurate conclusion had to do with God loving some of His children more than others based on how diligently they endeared themselves to Him.

This is basically what this teaching claimed: Jesus had a group of friends. The close friends were His twelve disciples; the closer friends were Peter, James, and John, BUT the closet friend, the person whom Jesus *really* loved, was John. Conclusion? Be like John and get close to Jesus. Sound familiar?

> **John 13:23**
> *Now there was leaning on Jesus' bosom one of His disciples, whom Jesus loved.*

Without any doubt, we knew God loved us intimately "the hour we first believed." We felt assured of His love. Then after years of being given the impression God had favorites and perhaps we were not yet one of them, the sense of being loved began to wane, until for some of us, it was nearly lost.

How we longed to return to knowing we were loved by God! This goal of aspiring to be the "disciple Jesus loved" clouded our perception and cast doubts on our relationship with Him. How would we ever get that close to God?

For God So Loved the World

This cannot be stated enough. God loves the entire world—yes even the most despicable among us. He died for us **before** we had an opportunity to prove ourselves worthy of His love.

> ### Titus 3:4-5
> *When the kindness and the love of God our Savior toward man appeared, ⁵ not by works of righteousness which we have done, but according to His mercy He saved us.*

We need to constantly remind ourselves that God's love is NOT merited by our works of righteousness. We can't earn His affection and we can't lose it. God simply loves us.

Individually Called by Grace but Equally Loved

Another reason we got side-tracked was we equated God's calling in ministry with the degree to which God loved someone. Take Enoch, for example. Was he the only human being on earth who "walked with God"? Unlikely. Yet God "took him" off the earth to be with Himself. Why? Because He loved Him more? Nothing in Scripture indicates this. The only hint we are given is that it had something to do with Enoch's *faith* in God.

> ### Hebrews 11:5
> *By **faith** Enoch was translated that he should not see death; and was not found, because God had translated him: for before his translation he had this testimony, that he pleased God.*

We might be tempted here to conclude, "Well, obviously Enoch pleased God. That's why God took him," but we would be missing the point being made by the writer of Hebrews.

Verse five says Enoch was translated "by faith," and to make sure we wouldn't miss the point, the writer informs us in verse six:

> *But without faith it is impossible to **please** him: for he that comes to God must believe that he is, and that he is a rewarder of those who diligently seek him.*

It was Enoch's *faith* that pleased God. Perhaps it was that as Enoch delighted in God's love so much that he one day said, "Oh, Lord, how I long to be with You," and the Lord said, "Come on up!"

We know that "Noah was a just man, perfect in his generations," and, "Noah walked with God," but considering that Scripture teaches that every inhabitant of the earth was completely corrupt, God's choices of whom to call to save the earth were rather limited. Still, "Noah found *grace* in the eyes of the Lord," and by *faith* Noah answered God's call.

Very little is said of Abraham before He was called. Yet God chose Abraham to father a nation (Gen.12:1-3).

God calls whom He wants, and it has nothing to do with our goodness or diligence.

Romans 9:14-16
What shall we say then? Is there unrighteousness with God? Certainly not! [15] *For He says to Moses, "I will have mercy on whomever I will have mercy, and I will have compassion on whomever I will have compassion."* [16] ***So then it is not of him who wills, nor of him who runs, but of God who shows mercy.***

As we continue down the list given in Hebrews 11, we see multiple examples of the grace of God extended and individuals responding in faith. It's perfectly acceptable to desire to be called by God, but we cannot earn that distinction by our good or diligent behavior.

Our chief example comes from a man who called himself "the chief of sinners," not because he was involved in sin at the time he wrote it, but because he had persecuted the church. He was making life miserable for believing Jews. Why would God call such a troublesome person as Paul? Was it because he was the disciple Jesus loved? Was it because he was a holy and righteous person?

This reminds me of the moment God called us into our current ministry. While sitting in church I was agonizing over the worship service. Not only were the song choices dirge-like, but there was one particular refrain in a song being repeated way too many times. My attitude was neither loving nor patient as evidenced by the super holy prayer I was (not) praying. My face was in my hands while I hoped no one would notice my fingers were in my ears. "God, please make them STOP," I prayed to myself.

Almost immediately, deep in my spirit, the Lord spoke to me and asked, "Are you willing?" Immediately, I was snapped out of my current frame of mind. God was talking to me! The sentence continued as I braced myself for the question, sensing it would change the course of our lives. I was already prepared to answer.

"Are you willing—to preach the gospel to the saved?" Knowing exactly what God meant, my immediate answer was "Yes, Lord. I am willing."

Stunned by the grace of God at that moment and the wonder of what this calling would look like (and with my hands still over my face but now in amazement), there was no way to deny what was happening. It was so intensely obvious God was speaking. Thankfully, upon sharing this experience with my husband, he received the calling as one for us both which led us to the delightful task of preaching good news to God's beloved kids so that they can be free.

Was this moment of God calling us given because God loved us more than everyone else in the sanctuary? It would have been foolish to think so. Was it because I was so mature, super-spiritual, and gracious? Obviously not! Was it because we were so well-connected in our denomination? Not in any way. Could it be because we were so influential and respected within the body of Christ? Hardly. Perhaps He called us because our parents were such powerhouses in Christ. No, again. Oh, I know! He called us because we are the disciples He loves. Nope. He just called us, and by faith, we answered. No one can boast if they are called, nor can they boast they answered. Paul wrote this verse about himself and his ministry.

1 Corinthians 15:10
But by the grace of God I am what I am, and His grace toward me was not in vain; but I labored more abundantly than they all, yet not I, but the grace of God which was with me.

The Disciple Jesus Loved

Many have pointed out that the only person who referred to John as "the disciple Jesus loved" was John himself. Was this because Jesus loved John the most? Let's think about that.

Jesus is never quoted as saying He loved John the most. Not even John said he was the disciple Jesus loved "the *most*," simply that Jesus loved him. Could it be, as others have surmised, that John recorded himself as loved by Jesus because he more acutely was aware of God's love for him?

Jesus loved all His disciples, didn't He? Or was it only to John He said, "As the Father loved Me, I also have loved you; abide in My love," (Jn. 15:9)? Did He say, "Greater love has no man than this that He lay down His life for John"? Or perhaps Jesus should have said, "This is My commandment that you love one another as I have loved John."

No. Jesus loved them all.

John 13:1
*Now before the **Feast** of the Passover, when Jesus knew that His hour had come that He should depart from this world to the Father, having loved His own who were in the world, **He loved them to the end**.*

It should also be noted that John referred to others as being loved by God.

John 11:5
Now Jesus loved Martha and her sister and Lazarus.

You, my friend, are also the disciple Jesus loves. He loved you when you were estranged from Him, and He loves you now. You are precious to Him. Let this truth sink into your heart. Can you say it?

☙ I am the disciple Jesus loves. ❧

"Jesus, we let go of any thought that you love some of us more than others. Today, we confess, 'We are the disciples Jesus loves.' You, Creator of Heaven and Earth, love us. You aren't ashamed of us if we have accomplished little in life. Your love isn't measured out to us based on some unidentifiable goodness within us. You simply love us. You love us just as much as You loved John. You love us as much as the Father loves You. Help us to know and believe You love us personally, deeply, and forever."

"As the Father loved Me,
I also have loved you;
abide in My love."

John 15:9

221

Continuing the Journey

Another devastating teaching which nullifies this glorious truth that God loves us is the misuse of these two verses. After reading the following, share your thoughts about this chapter.

> **John 15:14**
> *You are My friends **if** you do whatever I command you.*
> **John 15:10**
> ***If** you keep My commandments, you will abide in My love, just as I have kept My Father's commandments and abide in His love.*

The incorrect conclusion that is drawn from these verses is that we are only God's friends and loved by Him IF we keep His commandments. Completely ignoring the context of Jesus' statements, it is assumed Jesus is referring to every teaching of His while on earth as His commandments. We must pay attention to the context. Jesus had just given them a "new commandment" and it was to, "Love one another as I have loved you."

It was John who recorded the account of the giving of this new commandment in the Gospel of John who nearly 60 years later, confirmed what was meant by "His commandments."

> **1 John 3:22-23**
> *And whatever we ask we receive from Him, because we keep His commandments and do those things that are pleasing in His sight. 23 And **this is His commandment**: that we should **believe** on the name of His Son Jesus Christ and **love one another**, as He gave us commandment.*

One might be tempted to read verse 22 and shout, "See! I told you! We must keep the commandments and please Him." Yes, there are commandments in the New Covenant, and they are clearly expressed in the very next verse. Believe on the Son, and love each other. We don't do these things *so* God will love us, but *because* He loves us.

1 John 4:19 NASB
We love, because He first loved us.

Chapter 28

IMPROPER FOCUS

When this prodigal daughter returned to Christ, it seemed the angels in heaven were rejoicing. I felt the joy and love of God the Father at that moment so intensely. He might as well have appeared to me, put a ring on my finger, and had dinner prepared to celebrate my return. That's how special the moment of my homecoming was.

One day, about a year after my return to Jesus, I shared this joyous experience with a Christian friend. I said it seemed as if I'd done God a favor to believe in His Son—that He was so happy I'd come home. Rather than rejoice with me, this sentiment was summarily condemned, my friend becoming very offended at that thought.

How dare I think such a thing? Who did I think I was? What pride was surely in my heart! He told me in no uncertain terms that shame and humility would have been more appropriate. Amazingly, this did not dim my confidence—not at all. God's love and favor in my life was overwhelming.

Daily amazed by God's abiding love for me personally and His indwelling presence, there was nothing more beautiful than reflecting on this love. I'd see a feather on the street, pick it up and observe it had polka dots formed across its barbs as if they'd been stamped across the feather. "My Father did that," I'd say right out loud. "He left it as a sign He exists."

One day, while walking to our downtown Christian coffee house outreach, I started composing and singing a little song,

My Father made this world,
and everything in it.
My God made you and He made me.

He sent His only Son to
Live and die for us
My God loves you, and He loves me.

He gave up all He had and
Reached out to me.
Each day His love
Sets me free.[43]

Singing it to one of the brothers working at the coffee house that day turned out to be a bad idea because he was NOT impressed nor pleased with my creation—more annoyed with me than anything. Perhaps it was because it was such a *happy* tune.

I was learning that being *too* joyful or enthusiastic was not acceptable in our Christian community.

He said, "Why don't you sing about picking up your cross and *dying* with Jesus?" So, as a sweet little girl wanting to please her big brother, I instantly changed the words.

Pick up your cross and die with me.
You will also rise again with me.
Lay down your life and lose it.
You will also gain it one day.
He who seeks to save His life will
Lose it one day,
But He who forsakes all will gain.

---

[43] "My Father Made This World," a song by C. D. Hildebrand, Circa 1974

The melody was cheerful and went perfectly with the first song but sounded ridiculous with the second (which would have been better off with something more dismal). Somehow, it got out to the pastors I'd written a song, and they asked me to sing it for the church.

The song I'd written originally was for Christians and was about God being our Father and loving us. The song this brother provoked would only be appropriate to sing to non-Christians. They *need* to pick up their cross and die with Jesus. Christians don't need to die; we already did.

> **Romans 6:8-11**
> *Now if we **died** with Christ, we believe that we shall also live with Him, ⁹ knowing that Christ, having been raised from the dead, **dies no more**. Death no longer has dominion over Him. ¹⁰ For the death that He died, He died to sin **once** for all; but the life that He lives, He lives to God. ¹¹ **Likewise you also**, reckon yourselves to be **dead** indeed to sin, but **<u>alive to God</u>** in Christ Jesus our Lord.*

Why does it seem some leaders don't want new Christians to be happy about knowing they are loved by God for very long? Why do they feel they must quash their joy? Why do they consider the love new believers are feeling as a "honeymoon period"—something destined to soon fade away? Why does there seem to be an unspoken plot to bring the new believer riding high on God's love "down to earth" so that he can "go deeper" and learn to love the Lord his God with all their heart, and all his soul, and with all his might; which, by the way, he is quite supernaturally already doing?

If you want to stir up some dust, start talking about how happy you are to know God loves you. You might find this makes some Christians very uncomfortable. When posting such a comment one day, someone responded, "The problem with talking about how much God loves us is it puts the emphasis on *us* instead of God—always talking about what God does for *us* instead of what *we* can do for God."

How spiritual that would have sounded to us many years ago.

The complete opposite is true. When we focus on *His* love for us, we are giving glory to *Him*—*His* sacrifice, *His* promises, *His* provisions, *His* love. Let us just settle this issue definitively before continuing.

> **1 John 4:9-11**
> In **this** the love of God was manifested **toward us**, that God has sent His only begotten Son into the world, that we might **live** through Him. *10* In **this** is love, **not that we loved God,** but that **He** loved us and sent His Son to be the propitiation for our sins. *11* Beloved, if God so loved us, we also ought to love one another.

Love is about God loving us and sending His Son to die for our sins, NOT about us loving God. When we know how greatly our God loves us we quite naturally love Him. A born-again Christian does not need to be told to love God.

"Father, we love you with all of our hearts and souls and minds, not because You command us to do so, but because You made us new creations who cry out to You, 'Abba, Father.' We love You *because* You first loved us. For years we tried to prove our love for You through so many avenues. Help us, Father, to readjust our focus toward understanding the unending value of Your great love. Remove from within us any thoughts that seek to minimize putting an emphasis on Your love for us. Help us to rejoice in Your love for us and to be assured of it."

For this reason I bow my knees to the Father of our Lord Jesus Christ, 15 from whom the whole family in heaven and

*earth is named, 16 that He would grant you, according to the
riches of His glory, to be strengthened with might through His
Spirit in the inner man, 17 that Christ may dwell in your hearts
through faith; that you, being rooted and grounded in love,
18 may be able to comprehend with all the saints
what is the width and length and depth and height—
19 to know the love of Christ which passes knowledge;
that you may be filled with all the fullness of God.*

Ephesians 3:14-19

Continuing the Journey

1. How might focusing on God's love for you change your life?

2. As we finish up this section about teachings that nullify the
    glorious good news of God's excellent love for us, what
    other thoughts come to mind?

PART 5

Know and Believe

Chapter 29

NOTHING MORE THAN FEELINGS

*P*erhaps you've been in a church service, and it seemed everyone was getting blessed but you. Some were rejoicing, others weeping, but you sat still and felt nothing. Maybe you knelt at your seat to pray so no one would notice you were the only one not at the altar.

I went through a season like this. The message of grace we were preaching was awakening everyone who heard it just as it had done to us so many years before. It was such a joy to see the change God was bringing in each life, but for some reason, my feelings were flat. I ran the routine of ideas about why I might feel that way. Maybe I was simply weary. Perhaps I was just getting older. Eventually, my lack of emotions caused me to wonder if something might be *wrong* with me spiritually— or that God might be disappointed in me.

One afternoon when it seemed I might break down and cry about it, I turned to the Lord with my perplexing thoughts trusting that, just like always, He would help me figure it out. I was thinking He'd reveal the problem to me over time, but instead, in that instant and very clearly, He spoke to my heart and said, "Cathy, I'm not asking you to **feel** I love you. I'm asking you to **know and believe** the love I have for you." Instantly, the scripture below came to mind.

The peace that came over me at that moment was beautiful as I realized I was worried about what I *felt,* not about what I knew to be true—not about what I believed. I didn't doubt God's love for me. It was as if God reached down and found the precise knot to untie and unraveled my concerns. Instead of tears of sadness, came tears of joy. All was ok with God and me.

> **1 John 4:12-16**
> *No one has seen God at any time. If we love one another, God abides in us, and His love has been perfected in us. 13 By this we know that we abide in Him, and He in us, because He has given us of His Spirit. 14 And we have seen and testify that the Father has sent the Son as Savior of the world. 15 Whoever confesses that Jesus is the Son of God, God abides in him, and he in God. 16 **And we have known and believed the love that God has for us.** God is love, and he who abides in love abides in God, and God in him.*

The peace of this moment is what inspired the title of this book. No matter what we are going through and even if our feelings vary, God loves us. He isn't demanding we *feel* anything. He wants us to know and believe in His love. He has proven His love to us through the death of His Son. He wants us to receive this gift without doubting, no matter how things look or how we feel.

Some days when pondering God's love for me, it's difficult to bear its wonderfulness. Other days, I just live my life mostly with knowledge and faith in His love. It doesn't mean I love Him less or that He loves me less on any given day.

Feelings are a response to so many things—our health, hormones, what we think, and even just being bombarded by all the evil and negativity in our world wears us down. No matter what the reason is for why we feel how we do, we can live confidently in His love for us. He is not disappointed with us if we don't get emotional every time we think of His love. He knows all about what's going on in our hearts and lives. What pleases Him is our faith in His love.

You are worthy,
Worthy to be praised.
You are worthy
Each and every day.
You are wonderful,
Marvelous,
Amazing,
Mighty.

You are worthy
No matter how I feel.
You are worthy.
Your promises are real.
So, no matter what
I feel today
You're worthy,
Worthy to be praised.[44]

Continuing the Journey

1. Can you relate to the testimony above? Have you had a similar experience?

2. Why is it important not to rely on feelings when it comes to God's love for us and our relationship with Him?

---

[44] "Worthy to Be Praised," a song by C. D. Hildebrand during an extremely tumultuous storm in life, 2005

Chapter 30

BEHOLD

---

1 John 3:1
Behold what manner of love
the Father has bestowed on us!

*I*t's easy to skip over a word such as "behold" when reading Scripture, but let's take a closer look using Thayer's multi-level definition of the Greek word. If it's helpful, as you read the different aspects of how the word is applied in Scripture, picture in your mind how each definition would look if you or someone else were to act it out or read it out loud with expressive emphasis.

eidō
1) to see
   1a) to perceive with the eyes
   1b) to perceive by any of the senses
   1c) to perceive, notice, discern, discover
   1d) to see
   1e) to experience any state or condition
   1f) to see, i.e. have an interview with, to visit
2) to know
   2a) to know of anything
   2b) to know, i.e. get knowledge of, understand, perceive
   2c) to have regard for one, cherish, pay attention to

Behold, the love of God! See it with your eyes and all your senses. Perceive its value. Understand it. Discover His great love for you. Pay attention to it. Examine it. Gaze at it. Experience His love. Visit with it. Know it as a fact. Cherish it. Simply take the time to appreciate His astonishing love for you.

In Remembrance of His Love

Now, turn your eyes to the cross remembering the superiority of God's love compared to man's—a love that is continually commended and demonstrated to us by His death offered in love for us. Behold the love of God as He endured the punishment for our sin.

> ### 1 Corinthians 11:23-26
> *For I received from the Lord that which I also delivered to you: that the Lord Jesus on the same night in which He was betrayed took bread;* [24] *and when He had given thanks, He broke it and said, "Take, eat; this is My body which is broken for you; do this in remembrance of Me."* [25] *In the same manner He also took the cup after supper, saying, "This cup is the new covenant in My blood. This do, as often as you drink it, in remembrance of Me."*
> [26] *For as often as you eat this bread and drink this cup, you proclaim the Lord's death till He comes.*

Perceive the value of His sacrifice as you hold the bread and cup in your hands. Understand His great love for you as He was bruised. Pay attention to what He was doing for you. Examine what His death accomplished for you. Experience the love that was in His heart as His physical life slipped away. Be convinced of His affection for you. Treasure and cherish His grace. Do this in remembrance of His love for you.

Isaiah 53:4-6

Surely He has borne our griefs
And carried our sorrows;
Yet we esteemed Him stricken,
Smitten by God, and afflicted.
⁵ But He was wounded for our transgressions,
He was bruised for our iniquities;
The chastisement for our peace was upon Him,
And by His stripes we are healed.
⁶ All we like sheep have gone astray;
We have turned, every one, to his own way;
And the Lord has laid on Him the iniquity of us all.

What Manner of Love is This?

John asks us to behold what type of love is bestowed upon us. "Bestow" means "to give." We did nothing to deserve this love that caused Him to die for us and that now calls us children of God. Perceive the value of being a child of God. Those who were under the law were slaves. Those who are under grace are heirs. You are an heir of God, a full-fledged son. Behold the manner of love bestowed on you that you, yes, you would be called a child of God.

Romans 8:14-17

For as many as are led by the Spirit of God, these are sons of God.[45] ¹⁵ For you did not receive the spirit of bondage[46] again to fear, but you received the Spirit of adoption by whom we cry out, "Abba, Father." ¹⁶ The Spirit Himself bears witness with our spirit that we are children of God, ¹⁷ and if children, then heirs—heirs of God and joint heirs with Christ, if indeed we suffer with Him, that we may also be glorified together.

---

[45] In other words, the children of God ARE led by the Spirit of God.
[46] "Bondage" is in reference to the law.

Galatians 4:4-7
But when the fullness of the time had come, God sent forth His Son, born of a woman, born under the law, ⁵ to redeem those who were under the law, that we might receive the adoption as sons. ⁶ And because you are sons, God has sent forth the Spirit of His Son into your hearts, crying out, "Abba, Father!" ⁷ Therefore you are no longer a slave but a son, and if a son, then an heir of God through Christ.

During the time this chapter was being composed, we took a scenic drive to one of our favorite places, Bodega Bay[47]. As a child, our family often visited this location where I waded in the very cold and relatively calm waters—even unwittingly catching a baby Leopard shark with my hands one afternoon while swimming. We often camped overnight near Northern California beaches which nurtured in me a love of listening to the waves crashing upon the shore as the tide came in at night. Looking for sea shells and sand dollars was what every morning included which my mother seemed to delight in most of all. A trip to Bodega Bay always fills my heart and floods my mind with many treasured memories. It's one of those locations where one immediately relaxes upon arrival.

The roads were abnormally clear with our car seeming to be the only car on the road as we wound our way down the familiar route. We went to a favorite café built over the harbor waters for brunch and enjoyed watching the variety of birds and occasional sea otter floating on the surface. Next, we walked on the beach during low tide and relished in the ambience as we picked up what few shells were left that hadn't been completely destroyed by hungry birds. To my delight, I found a couple feathers which when all of their parts flowed together

---

[47] Bodega Bay is fishing village and tourist location about an hour and a half north of San Francisco, California. It was the location for Alfred Hitchcock's film, "The Birds."

formed stripes. How wonderful of God to speak to us through His creation. "I am here, and I love you," He seemed to say.

When it appeared we would start our journey home, David delighted me by asking, "Do you want to go to Bodega Head?"[48]

"You won't have to pull my leg on that one," I said, then corrected myself, "I mean, twist my arm," and we laughed because it's not uncommon for me to get these types of expressions mixed up.

When we arrived, it was very windy and cold, but the view was stunning. Feeling so energized by it all, we climbed up a short trail to get an even better view. Not only was the coast-line breathtaking, but tiny little spring flowers were dotting the landscape of the cliff which was covered in a variety of green grasses and ice plant which was blooming its yellow daisy-like flowers.

When the time arrived to return home, I decided to take in the view just one more time, and while covering the 180-degree view I tried to memorize it all from one side to the other. Quite unexpectedly, a word came into my mind which brought tears to my eyes.

"Behold!" the familiar voice seemed to encourage me. So, I looked again and was surprised there was more to see. From the far-off horizon my eyes were drawn to the height of the bright blue skies which had broken through the clouds. The enormous rock formations scattered about the coastline for miles with the waves crashing upon them came into focus. Birds of different varieties were sunning on the cliffs nearby, and in the distance, a large group of seals were bobbing up and down in the rhythmic flow of the waves. Then I pondered the depth of the sea and the life that surely was hidden below. My heart filled with wonder as I remembered this verse.

Ephesians 3:14-19
For this reason I bow my knees to the Father of our Lord Jesus Christ, [15] from whom the whole

---

[48] Bodega Head is a very high cliff overlooking part of the rocky Northern California coastline near the entrance to the bay.

*family in heaven and earth is named, [16] that He would grant you, according to the riches of His glory, to be strengthened with might through His Spirit in the inner man, [17] that Christ may dwell in your hearts through faith; **that you, being rooted and grounded in love, [18] may be able to comprehend with all the saints what is the width and length and depth and height— [19] to know the love of Christ which passes knowledge; that you may be filled with all the fullness of God.***

Brothers and sisters in Christ, just as we can appreciate more deeply anything in nature by looking at it more closely, God wants us to carefully examine His great love for us. He wants us to enjoy the width and length of His love—a love that includes the whole world but focuses on us, His beloved children. Consider the heights and depths of His excellent, enduring love. What kind of love could encompass the worst of sinners while individually nurturing and comforting His own?

Behold, the manner of love the Father has given to us! Simply take a moment any time of the day to ponder the vastness of His love for you personally. Allow yourself to be amazed by it. Know the truth of it. Let us believe it and receive it even though we could never earn such immense affection which we will be discovering continually during this life and in the life to come.

"Father, we pray the prayer Paul prayed for the Ephesian believers. May we be rooted and grounded in Your love and be able to comprehend the width and length and depth and height of Your love for us. Help us to know Your love which passes knowledge so we may be filled with Your fullness."

O Lord, our Lord,
How excellent is Your name in all the earth,
Who have set Your glory above the heavens!
[3] When I consider Your heavens, the work of Your fingers,

239

The moon and the stars, which You have ordained,
⁴ What is man that You are mindful of him,
And the son of man that You visit him?
⁵ For You have made him a little lower than the angels,
And You have crowned him with glory and honor.
⁶ You have made him to have dominion
over the works of Your hands;
You have put all things under his feet,
⁷ All sheep and oxen—
Even the beasts of the field,
⁸ The birds of the air,
And the fish of the sea
That pass through the paths of the seas.
⁹ O Lord, our Lord,
How excellent is Your name in all the earth!

Psalm 8:1,3-9

Continuing the Journey

1. What thoughts come to mind when you "behold" the love of God?

2. Sometimes it is beneficial to look back on the many times God has shown His love to us throughout our lives. If you'd like, record some of those experiences here to remind yourself of His goodness toward you.

Chapter 31

SATISFIED GOD

**In the heart of every believer
❧ resides the desire to love and please God. ❧**

Galatians 4:6
*And because you are sons, God has sent forth
the Spirit of His Son into your hearts, crying
out, "Abba, Father!"*

*A*ll Christians want to please God. He sent the Spirit of His Son into our hearts so just as any young child would, we long to please our Father and yearn for His approval. This desire to please Him is so intense in new believers, we often begin our walk with Him by asking, "HOW do I please God?" Most of us, not yet being well-versed in Scripture will readily receive the advice of more mature Christians as to what pleasing God looks like. Sadly, the answers given to this question often send the new believer down the same dead-end road which their counselors are so diligently jogging—sidelining grace and faith and emphasizing law and works.

A God Who Can Be Pleased

For many years we endeavored diligently to love God by doing whatever our pastors told us would please Him. The desire to satisfy God was so great, and our pastors were such godly and kind people, it seemed natural to take the path they were taking. Over the years, however, like hamsters on a spinning wheel, we never got to where we thought we were going. There was always more we could do. We were the proverbial muzzled ox treading the corn—seeing the harvest, but never able to partake. We just kept pulling the plow hoping one day we'd see the fruit of it.

Yet perhaps there was hope! Shortly after we became home mission pastors, my husband shared with me something he'd heard previously at a conference for youth pastors that had stuck in his mind. He told me one of the speakers said something that really touched him. "Our God is a God who can be pleased," he'd said.

How sad it is that this was a foreign concept to the two of us. Maybe it was because God had become to us like a friendly ogre gobbling up our efforts but always wanting more. The idea we could actually *please* God at some point delighted us both for many weeks, so much so that I wrote this little song.

> *You are the Lord of my life,*
> *And I want to make you happy.*
> *You're Lord of my life.*
> *How I long to see you smile.*
> *There is nothing*
> *More important in my life*
> *Than to know that I bring*
> *Pleasure to your heart.*[49]

Yet something quite crucial eluded us—HOW? How on God's green earth could we actually please God?

The List

So, theoretically, God *could* be pleased, but we were completely oblivious as to what "more" it would take to satisfy Him.

---

[49] "You Are the Lord of My Life," a song by C. D. Hildebrand, circa 1982

We assumed it would certainly still involve completing the ever-growing list of spiritual disciplines which by then encompassed every aspect of our lives. Please bear with me as I elaborate once again.

Of course, there were the basics—pray an hour daily and read ten chapters from the Bible each day. Prayer included worship, thanksgiving, intercession, and an occasional prayer for our own lives. The Bible was to be studied, meditated upon, memorized, sung, and put on our walls. David graduated from Bible School, and I graduated via correspondence. We both became licensed and then ordained ministers (because going into full-time ministry *was the ultimate proof of one's love for and dedication to God*).

In addition to prayer and Bible study, we needed to "be holy as He is holy" which to us meant abstaining from any unholy activity, thought, word, and deed. Wearing anything but a dress to church was not acceptable and that dress had to be overly modest. We did not go to movies. We didn't own a television. We didn't listen to anything but Christian music, and we'd thrown away all the secular music albums we possessed. We didn't go to secular concerts. We only read Christian books, except for required university textbooks. We didn't dance—God forbid, except a little bit in church during worship. All of this was our way of trying to please God. It wasn't done out of fear of losing eternal life. We weren't in a cult. We *chose* to live like this because we thought this was pleasing to God, and we thought that by doing these things we would become increasingly holy.

We needed to make sure we were "right with God" which not only meant we lived a sinless life but completed the list of do's and don'ts. We were to share Jesus with everyone everywhere we went. We were to give at least ten percent to the church and to "give sacrificially" which in our situation meant giving what we really didn't have to give.

Money wasn't enough. It was expected we would give our time. For those seeking to be in ministry, secular careers and even secular education were regarded as "self-serving." Only pursuing ministry would suffice.

Even though we were in ministry, there was that little unspoken stipulation about being *successful* in ministry. Publicly, it was stated that what God expected was that each minister be faithful, even if the numbers were few, but locally and within our denomination it was reinforced that "church growth" **mattered**. Church growth seminars abounded. Those with increasing members were granted great esteem within our denomination and those whose congregations remained small were left to feel inadequate with a simple pat on the head (so to speak).

Being a good spouse was a big one; but, just as we felt we couldn't please God, we had little confidence we could be good enough for each other either, and since there were so many enjoyments on our list of don'ts, there was little left we could do to enjoy each other's company.

Being an excellent Christian parent was also on the list. This meant being a good disciplinarian, teaching our kids the word at home, bringing them to church regularly, encouraging them to be saved and get baptized .

We read multiple books on having a good marriage and being good parents because being a successful family was crucial to pleasing God, and we were taught if our family wasn't nearly perfect, we had no right being in ministry. Each book had its own list of disciplines which only weighed us down further, setting such high standards no one could possibly fully complete them (but we tried anyway). At one point, I completely stopped reading Christian books.

Interestingly enough, this long list which we accumulated over the years for our own lives was thankfully not something we passed on to our children. We spoke to them of God's love for them and extended much more grace to them than we did to ourselves. This is because my mother raised me with such grace and love that we determined to follow her example. We agreed about loving our children overtly and speaking good words over their lives. We did not yell at our children nor insult them ever—not even in a tease. The dichotomy couldn't have been more pronounced. Our kids were experiencing the love and grace of God that we were not.

Without realizing it,
☙ we were protecting our children ❧
from what was killing us.

Time and money management were also heavily emphasized because it did not please God to waste either. Each minute of the day was to be planned out and each dollar spent was to glorify God in some way.

As we began to understand the grace of God and He showed us we had taken a wrong turn in our walk with Him, we disposed of the list item by item as God gave us revelation. However, we observed that within the church the list continued to expand to more extreme measures so much so that one must wonder what would be next. Shall we beat ourselves with chains, crawl over glass and gravel, deny ourselves of necessities to prove our love for God? Shall we give our bodies to be burned—wait just one minute!

1 Corinthians 13:1-3
Though I speak with the tongues of men and of angels, but ***have not love****, I have become sounding brass or a clanging cymbal.*
² And though I have the gift of prophecy, and understand all mysteries and all knowledge, and though I have all faith, so that I could remove mountains, but have not love, I am nothing.
³ And though I bestow all my goods to feed the poor, and though I give my body to be burned, but have not love, it profits me nothing.

Previously, I read this portion of Scripture in a completely different light. What I heard was, "No matter how much you do for God, if you don't act like the list that follows describing love, then you are nothing,"—emphasis on being *nothing*, of never satisfying God.

Now, I see it in a completely different light—what good does it do to be super-spiritual and make extreme sacrifices if we do not know God's love for us? If we do not have love—God's love, we are nothing, and all the works we're doing in no way profit us.

Although we were deeply entrenched in error, God saw our hearts, and He knew that with all our beings we were endeavoring to please Him and show Him our love. Tragically, we'd been led down the well-trodden dead-end road of justification by works. If someone had told us we were trying to be justified by works, we would have greatly quarreled with him. We saw everything we did as our way of loving God with all of our heart, our souls, and our might. Our only desire was to please God. Our motives were pure. We weren't trying to exalt ourselves by keeping this list. We thought this was how we were to exalt God.

Never mind that none of our efforts were working in the slightest. We didn't feel closer to God. We never really felt quite right with Him. We were always looking for that new spiritual discipline that would bring us closer. We longed to know His love but didn't really. We were more than miserable; we were nearly dead. The worst part about this is that instead of acknowledging that what we were doing wasn't helping, we thought the list to which we were clinging for righteousness to be the *cure* for our growing wretchedness. So, we'd apply the "cure" for our agony which was actually the cause of it. We were drinking poison we thought was medicine, and it just kept making us increasingly sick.

Without Faith

Hebrews 11:6
And without faith it is impossible to please Him, for he who comes to God must believe that He is and that He is a rewarder of those who seek Him.

Since reading our Bibles daily was on our list, we had repeatedly read the above verse, but we totally missed its importance. In my recent writings, I've emphasized the flipside—that with faith it *is* possible to please God; and of course, this is true. Yet the author of Hebrews puts it in the negative, certainly for some reason. *Without* faith, it is *impossible* to please God. There is no other way to please God but by faith. We were trying to please God by law through works, instead of by grace through faith.

It is impossible to please God without faith, so that is why we never felt God was satisfied. It didn't help that our view of "faith" increasingly had become viewed as us trying really hard to believe. Faith became a work along with all the other things we were diligently doing. We just kept dragging ourselves down the same ancient path of righteousness by self-effort never realizing God was pleased with us the first day we put our faith in Jesus.

Which Came First

Did we save ourselves? No. Can we save ourselves? No. When He comes, is there something we will be able to do to save ourselves? No. We were, are, and will be saved because of what God provided *for* us, namely, salvation by faith in His only Son's sacrifice. NEVER is anyone saved by keeping the law or doing good works or by "making Jesus Lord." He is Lord—believing that, is what saves us.

> ### Ephesians 2:8-10
> *For by grace you have been saved through faith, and that not of yourselves; it is the gift of God, ⁹ **not of works**, lest anyone should boast. ¹⁰ For we are His workmanship, created in Christ Jesus for good works, which God prepared beforehand that we should walk in them.*

We were created *for* good works, not by them, and good works have nothing to do with making a list and checking it twice (Eph. 2:10). How can keeping a list be a good work? Our list helped no one. It was all about *us*, what *we* had to do so *we* might please God. We never saw how self-centered our religion was until we understood that this life is all about what Jesus did for us and not about what we do for Jesus—that living in this knowledge causes us to do more than ever before the good works for which we've been created, and that those good works benefit others.

Consider again the list of heroes in Hebrews 11. Formerly, we read the chapter thinking of the great things these people did for God, but the focus isn't on what they *did*, it is on what they *believed*.

> By **faith** Abel offered a better sacrifice.
> By **faith** Enoch pleased God.
> By **faith** Noah prepared an arc.
> By **faith** Abraham obeyed.
> By **faith** Sarah conceived.
> By **faith** Abraham offered up Isaac.
> By **faith** Isaac blessed Jacob and Esau.
> By **faith** Jacob blessed his twelve sons.
> By **faith** Moses forsook Egypt.
> By **faith** they passed through the Red Sea.
> By **faith** the walls of Jericho fell.
> By **faith** Rahab received the spies.

All of these people DID something, but it wasn't the doing that pleased God, it was their faith that *He* would do something. Can walking around a city cause the walls to fall down? No, but faith in God can. Could Daniel keep hungry lions from eating him alive? No, but faith in God did. Can the weak make themselves strong? No. Can three young men walk into a fiery furnace that just killed the men who threw them in and be completely untouched? No. By faith they were saved.

> **Daniel 3:16-18**
> Shadrach, Meshach, and Abed-Nego answered and said to the king, "O Nebuchadnezzar, we have no need to answer you in this matter. 17 If that is the case, our God whom we serve is able to deliver us from the burning fiery furnace, and **He will deliver us from your hand, O king**. 18 But if not, let it be known to

you, O king, that we do not serve your gods,
nor will we worship the gold image which you
have set up."

Pleased with His Creation

Genesis 1:31
Then God saw everything that He had made,
and indeed it was very good.

After six days of creating, God looked at what He created and was pleased with His work. Perhaps you know the joy of being able to create something. Let's say you are a carpenter; then you know the satisfaction that comes when you finish a piece you designed. Maybe you are a chef and you can identify with the joy of coming up with a new menu item that is perfect in every way. Any type of artist also knows the joy of creating a work of art and feeling pleased with it.

Parents also experience this joy as they watch their children growing up. That is just a small hint of what God felt when He created the earth. It all made sense and was in perfect order. The work of creation pleased Him, and He was satisfied.

This beautiful landscape was destroyed by sin, but God had a plan to restore man by sending His Son to pay the penalty for Adam's transgression. In Christ, we were recreated.

2 Corinthians 5:17
Therefore, if anyone is in Christ, he is a new
creation; old things have passed away; behold,
all things have become new.

He not only recreated us, but He is right now transforming us into the image of His dear Son—working in us both to will and to do of His good pleasure (2 Cor. 3:18, Phil. 2:13). This is the rest we find in Jesus. He does all of the work we could not possibly accomplish.

Levi's Quilt

For each of our ten grandchildren, I made a very special quilt. Each one is completely unique as are each one of them. When we found out our second grandchild was on the way, it was time to tackle quilt number two. As soon as the gender was revealed and the nursery colors determined, preparation got underway. I poured over quilting books searching for just the right design. As I did not yet own an abundance of scraps, days were spent visiting multiple sewing stores searching for the dozens of fabrics needed for a baby quilt which would have hundreds of pieces. Much love and planning went into what colors looked best with each other so the finished quilt would look fantastic. Then came the measuring and cutting which took many days until finally, the pieces were sewn together to form the many squares which were then joined to make bigger squares. After making a patchwork border, the time came to hand-sew the whole quilt together.

It seemed to take forever just to sew the face of the quilt, but finally, it was finished. Before ironing it in preparation to sew the front to the back by hand, I laid it on a flat surface to inspect my work. Suddenly, my eyes began to well with tears. The vision for the blanket I'd created was exactly what I wanted, and my heart was glowing with joy and satisfaction. It was beautiful.

I began to wonder if perhaps my feelings might be laced with a little too much pride in my creation. How could I get so emotional about a baby blanket? Then it happened.

A thought came into my heart as if God had

been watching me the whole time. "That's how I feel when I look at you, Cathy," He said. "I am pleased with the work I'm doing in your life." Then the tears that had been welling up in my eyes overflowed, and I began to weep tears of joy.

God was pleased with me! My life brought Him pleasure, and even though He did it all, there was nothing more important to me than knowing I brought Him joy. Just as the blanket itself had nothing to do with it being so beautiful, I had nothing to do with what God was accomplishing in me. He was teaching me how to live by grace through faith, and that faith allowed God to complete the work He started.

When the world looks at us, they see only our obvious flaws. They just see our outward shells and assume the shell is who we are. God, however, sees us—the ones He's been designing since we were in the womb. He sees our hearts and He not only loves us, but He is pleased because we believe in Him.

God is satisfied with the work He is doing in your life. He is beaming with pride at who you are becoming. God sees the new creation He has made you and He sees ahead to the completed work and indeed, behold, it is "very good." Even if you are still very rough around the edges, He isn't alarmed. He has faith in His power to transform you.

Psalm 139:14-18
I will praise You, for I am fearfully and wonderfully made;
Marvelous are Your works,
And that my soul knows very well.
15 My frame was not hidden from You,
When I was made in secret,
And skillfully wrought in the lowest parts of the earth.
16 Your eyes saw my substance, being yet

unformed.
And in Your book they all were written,
The days fashioned for me,
When as yet there were none of them.
[17] How precious also are Your thoughts to me,
O God!
How great is the sum of them!
[18] If I should count them, they would be more in
number than the sand;
When I awake, I am still with You.

"God, the thought that simply believing in You is what pleases You touches our hearts so deeply. You aren't asking us to perform spiritual gymnastics, to run spiritual marathons, or lift spiritual weights. You are simply asking us to believe in Your goodness and love, to reach out in faith to You when facing troubles, and rest in who You are and in what You provide for us. What is still lacking in our personal development is for You to accomplish. Thank-You that You are working in us both to do and to will of Your good pleasure. You love us, and we trust in Your love."

I thank my God upon every remembrance of you,
[4] always in every prayer of mine
making request for you all with joy,
[5] for your fellowship in the gospel
from the first day until now,
[6] being confident of this very thing,
that He who has begun a good work in you
will complete it until the day of Jesus Christ.

Philippians 1:3-6

Continuing the Journey

1. At this time in your life, do you think you are trying to please God by what you do and don't do, or do you recognize that it is your faith in Him that pleases Him? Describe your journey.

2. The Bible uses the terms "dead works" and "good works"? How might you describe to someone what the differences are between them? Might it be possible for one action to be both a dead work or a good work depending on the motivation behind it? Can you think of examples?

3. Have you ever looked in the mirror and seen what God sees? Describe your thoughts.

4. The book of Hebrews was written to encourage them to forsake law righteousness and embrace the righteousness which comes by believing in Jesus. Read the following verse. What is the rest we have? What does it mean to cease from our works?

    ### Hebrews 4:9-10
    There remains therefore a rest for the people of God. [10] For he who has entered His rest has himself also ceased from his works as God did from His.

Chapter 32

GOD IS LOVE

O ne of the most well-known passages about love is 1 Corinthians 13:4-8. It has been memorized by millions and quoted at just as many weddings.

> **1 Corinthians 13:4-8**
> Love suffers long and is kind; love does not envy; love does not parade itself, is not puffed up; ⁵ does not behave rudely, does not seek its own, is not provoked, thinks no evil; ⁶ does not rejoice in iniquity, but rejoices in the truth; ⁷ bears all things, believes all things, hopes all things, endures all things. ⁸ Love never fails.

What a beautiful expression of love. Most people see this passage as a fit description of the love we should have for each other, and truly it is. Even though one's experience in marriage and other relationships may have fallen woefully short, it remains the desired standard of love.

While many translations of this verse begin with, "Love is patient. Love is kind," it is noteworthy that in the Greek, instead of defining what love *is* and isn't, the passage describes love in terms of what love *does* and doesn't do (as in the above translation). This distinction is significant because when it comes to God's love toward us and the love He asks us to have toward each other, the emphasis is always on what is *done* rather than what is *felt*, even to the point of giving one's life.

> **John 15:12-13**
> *This is My commandment, that you love one another as I have loved you.* ¹³ *Greater love has no one than this, than to **lay down one's life** for his friends.*
>
> **Matthew 25:34-40**
> *Then the King will say to those on His right hand, 'Come, you blessed of My Father, inherit the kingdom prepared for you from the foundation of the world:* ³⁵ *for I was hungry and you **gave** Me food; I was thirsty and you **gave** Me drink; I was a stranger and you **took** Me in;* ³⁶ *I was naked and you **clothed** Me; I was sick and you **visited** Me; I was in prison and you **came** to Me.'*
> ³⁷ *"Then the righteous will answer Him, saying, 'Lord, when did we see You hungry and **feed** You, or thirsty and **give** You drink?* ³⁸ *When did we see You a stranger and **take** You in, or naked and **clothe** You?* ³⁹ *Or when did we see You sick, or in prison, and **come** to You?'* ⁴⁰ *And the King will answer and say to them, 'Assuredly, I say to you, **inasmuch as you did it to one of the least of these My brethren, you did it to Me.'***

In any human relationship, someone might say he loves you, but, "Actions speak louder than words," right? If someone loves us, their behavior toward us will be loving. Thankfully, God's love for us isn't simply *stated*; it is demonstrated by what He did, what He does, and what He will do.

God is Love

I honestly don't remember when the light bulb went on for me as it has for so many others, that since God is love (1 Jn. 4:8), then He, or if you prefer, His love, is everything described in 1 Corinthians 13:4-8.

It's embarrassing to admit that for many years my image of God did not match the descriptions in this passage which is likely why the correlation remained hidden from me for so long. This description of love seemed to be more about what was expected of *our* character and how *we* were supposed to behave. In an odd sense in my mind, God got a pass. Maybe I thought that since He was God, He could misbehave, though I seriously doubt I would have ever said such a thing publicly.

Thankfully, this passage is not only a message to us about us. It is also a representation of who God is and how His love is manifested. Shall He not be at least as loving as He asks us to be? Indeed—He far exceeds what we could ever imitate.

Let us now consider some of the expressions of love in the above verses in light of God fitting the description to help us better comprehend God's love for us.

> ### Ephesians 5:1-2
> *Therefore be **imitators of God** as dear children.*
> *2 And **walk in love**, as Christ also has loved us and given Himself for us, an offering and a sacrifice to God for a sweet-smelling aroma.*

God's Love Suffers Long

To be patient is to be longsuffering.[50] Admittedly, my image of God, although I'm sure I never put it into words, was that He had a rather short fuse. When taking into consideration the flood, for example, I envisioned a God who'd had enough of man's rebellion! Consider, though, that God endured the evil of mankind on the earth for nearly 1,700 years before he decided

---

[50] The two Greek words are used interchangeably.

to destroy its inhabitants and only after "*every* intent of the thoughts of man's heart was *only* evil *continually.*" Furthermore, it took Noah 100 years to build the ark. Knowing Noah was a "preacher of righteousness" it makes sense that as he built, he preached, and yet they refused to hear.

> **1 Peter 3:18-20**
> *For Christ also suffered once for sins, the just for the unjust, that He might bring us to God, being put to death in the flesh but made alive by the Spirit, [19] by whom also He went and preached to the spirits in prison[51], [20] who formerly were disobedient, when once the **Divine longsuffering waited** in the days of Noah, while the ark was being prepared, in which a few, that is, eight souls, were saved through water.*

When our patience is spent, how much longer can *we* endure? God patiently waited while Noah built the ark, enduring those who despised and continued to reject Him. He did this for the purpose of saving a remnant of humanity and the animals he'd so lovingly created so that from Noah a Redeemer could come. In the same way, God is waiting now.

Another factor that contributed to my view of God as impatient came from the accounts during the Old Covenant in which God's wrath was rightfully kindled against the unbelieving Israelites. God seemed like an impatient even irrational God, doling out swift punishments to all who crossed Him even needing Moses to hold Him back. Yet as previously stated, the children of Israel were under a covenant which included both blessings and condemnation. God dealt with them according to that covenant.

---

[51] For an explanation of what is meant by "spirits in prison," see <u>Hard Sayings of the Bible</u>, Walter C. Kaiser Jr., Peter H. Davids, F. F. Bruce, and Manfred T. Brauch, Intervarsity Press

> **2 Corinthians 3:7-11**
> But if the **ministry of death**, written and engraved on stones, was glorious, so that the children of Israel could not look steadily at the face of Moses because of the glory of his countenance, which glory was passing away, *8* how will the ministry of the Spirit not be more glorious? *9* For if the **ministry of condemnation** had glory, the ministry of righteousness exceeds much more in glory. *10* For even what was made glorious had no glory in this respect, because of the glory that excels. *11* For if what is passing away was glorious, what remains is much more glorious.

Even so, God's desire was to pour out His blessings upon them. He did mighty miracles for them, sent prophets to warn them, even while they turned to idols again and again. He sent them into captivity, but as He promised, He delivered them out of it. He sent them times of refreshing, but they continually tried Him. He sent His only Son to redeem them, but most of them refused Him. Even so, we can hear His longing for them in these words of Jesus.

> **Matthew 23:37**
> "O Jerusalem, Jerusalem, the one who kills the prophets and stones those who are sent to her! How often I wanted to gather your children together, as a hen gathers her chicks under her wings, but you were not willing!"

Under the Law, reward and punishment were crucial to guide them (just as most parents lovingly train their own children) because they did not have God's laws written on their hearts. We, who accepted God's gift of righteousness, who live under the New Covenant only, who have new hearts and whose sins are remembered no more, need not concern ourselves with reward and punishment. Jesus paid the penalty for our sins by fulfilling the requirements of the law (Rom. 4:3-4). His death initiated a New Covenant and nullified the Old (Heb. 8:13). We are *only* blessed and need not be concerned about the justified wrath of God.

> ### 1 Thessalonians 5:8-10
> *But let us who are of the day be sober, putting on the breastplate of faith and love, and as a helmet the hope of salvation. ⁹ For God **did not appoint us to wrath**, but to obtain salvation through our Lord Jesus Christ, ¹⁰ who died for us, that whether we wake or sleep, we should live together with Him.*

Obviously, the world continues in rebellion against God, and things will get worse before the end comes.

> ### 2 Timothy 3:1-5
> *But know this, that in the last days perilous times will come: ² For men will be lovers of themselves, lovers of money, boasters, proud, blasphemers, disobedient to parents, unthankful, unholy, ³ unloving, unforgiving, slanderers, without self-control, brutal, despisers of good, ⁴ traitors, headstrong, haughty, lovers of pleasure rather than lovers of God, ⁵ having a form of godliness but denying its power. And from such people turn away!*

Yet He patiently waits so that all who believe in Him will not perish but have everlasting life even though the inhabitants of this earth commit evil and hate good. God sees all the injustice on the earth. He sees every murder, every crime, every abduction. It isn't that He has changed His mind about anything He has spoken concerning His final return to judge the world, but He is patiently waiting for as many as possible to believe and be saved.

> **2 Peter 3:9**
> *The Lord is not slack concerning His promise,
> as some count slackness, but is **longsuffering**
> toward us, **not willing that any should perish**
> but that all should come to repentance.*

Our God is "the God of patience." Patience is who He is, and, more importantly, it is what he does. When we fall short of who He has designed us to be, He is patient with us. When we are impatient with ourselves, He is still patient. When we get off-track, He patiently works in our hearts so we will want to do His will.

> **Romans 15:4-5**
> *For whatever things were written before were
> written for our learning, that we through the
> patience and comfort of the Scriptures might
> have hope. ⁵ Now may the **God of patience**
> and comfort grant you to be like-minded toward
> one another, according to Christ Jesus.*

Perhaps it is because human beings generally are not patient, that we assume God to be the same. Again, let us not compare God's feelings with those of mankind. Rather, let us see the *contrast*. God is patient toward all—even His enemies (*unlike* most humans), and He beckons us to follow His example.

God's Love is Being Kind

The word for "kind" in 1 Corinthians 13:4 means "to *show oneself useful*, that is, *act benevolently:* - be kind."[52] It comes from the word **chrēstos** in the Greek which means, among other things, gracious. We can see in the examples below, that this word is translated as "easy, kind, goodness, and

---

[52] Strong

gracious." As you read these verses, allow your conception of "kind" to expand.

> **Matthew 11:30**
> *For My yoke is **easy** (kind) and My burden is light."*
>
> **Luke 6:32-35**
> *"But if you love those who love you, what credit is that to you? For even sinners love those who love them. [33] And if you do good to those who do good to you, what credit is that to you? For even sinners do the same. [34] And if you lend to those from whom you hope to receive back, what credit is that to you? For even sinners lend to sinners to receive as much back. [35] But love your enemies, do good, and lend, hoping for nothing in return; and your reward will be great, and you will be sons of the Most High. For He is **kind** to the unthankful and evil.[36] Therefore be merciful, just as your Father also is merciful.*
>
> **Romans 2:4**
> *Or do you despise the riches of His goodness, forbearance, and longsuffering, not knowing that the **goodness** (kindness) of God leads you to repentance?*
>
> **1 Peter 2:3**
> *If indeed you have tasted that the Lord is **gracious** (kind).*
>
> **Ephesians 4:32**
> *And be **kind** to one another, tenderhearted, forgiving one another, even as God in Christ forgave you.*

When someone is kind, they do good for others; they are gracious (giving). God is kind. He provides rain and sunshine for all. Jesus encourages us to be kind as God is kind—to be gracious to all, including those who do not deserve it.

Our tendency is to shun those who do not love us as we think they should. We don't want to risk being hurt again, so we bar them from our lives feeling justified in doing so, but God's kindness reaches out and does good even to His enemies.

God's Love Does Not Envy

The meaning of "envy" (jealousy) is used in Scripture in both a negative and positive sense each originating from the idea of an earnest zeal. It is used in the positive sense in that God is jealous for us. He doesn't want to share us with any other gods. In the Old Testament when referring to God as being jealous, it primarily had to do with Israel worshipping idols.

We see this same sentiment expressed in Acts 15. The Jerusalem council of elders were debating whether the Gentiles needed to be circumcised and keep the law of Moses. Their conclusions were that they did not need to keep the law of Moses but were to still refrain from sexual immorality and any association with idol worship.

Jealously is also positively expressed by Paul when speaking to the Corinthians who were following after teachers who were spreading false doctrine. Paul lovingly taught them, but others with less than noble motives and false teachings had infiltrated the flock to subjugate them, even to the point of degrading Paul.

> ### 2 Corinthians 11:2-4
> *For I am **jealous** for you with **godly jealousy**.*
> *For I have betrothed you to one husband, that*
> *I may present you as a chaste virgin to Christ.*
> *³ But I fear, lest somehow, as the serpent*
> *deceived Eve by his craftiness, so your minds*
> *may be corrupted from the simplicity that is in*
> *Christ. ⁴ For if he who comes preaches another*
> *Jesus whom we have not preached, or if you*
> *receive a different spirit which you have not*
> *received, or a different gospel which you have*

not accepted—you may well put up with it!

Paul's heart was jealous for them. He cared for them as his own children in the Lord and was pleading with them to remain faithful to Jesus and not follow these charlatans.

Those who have been married also understand the importance of a healthy dose of jealously. Many of us have experienced someone else flirting with one's spouse, and that sense of jealousy rises. It is correct for us not to want to share our spouse with anyone else in any way. It is why we promise to keep ourselves "only unto" that person.

So, yes, God is a jealous God in that He does not want to share us with empty idols or those who would seek to harm us, and we ourselves are jealous for our families and friends, but there is a negative jealousy that manifests itself in selfish ambition and covetousness. When someone resents instead of congratulating the success of another or works to take away from someone what is rightfully his, this is negative jealousy. God does not do this. His motives are always pure. Just as a good parent beams with pride at the success of his child, so God is happy for us when we succeed.

God's Love Does Not Parade Itself

When contemplating this characteristic of exalting oneself, we think of it in human terms because in our world, tooting one's horn is commonplace. Even though we might criticize those who take part in this folly, we often indulge in it ourselves.

It is impossible to think of God as someone who waltzes about bragging of His accomplishments. Now, His accomplishments are worthy of praise, which is why we praise Him, but His focus is on building us.

God's Love is Not Puffed Up

People are full of pride. This is obvious, but God isn't prideful. He has no need to exalt Himself as He is already and will forever be supreme. Yet Jesus set aside His high position and humbled Himself by coming to earth in the form of man and by dying a humiliating death on the cross for us. He could have called for angels to rescue Him from this shameful torture and death, but instead He carried away our sorrows, sicknesses, and sins (Matt. 26:53).

> **Philippians 2:5-8**
> *Let this mind be in you which was also in Christ Jesus, ⁶ (AMP: this verse only) who, although He existed in the form and unchanging essence of God [as One with Him, possessing the fullness of all the divine attributes—the entire nature of deity], did not regard equality with God a thing to be grasped or asserted [as if He did not already possess it, or was afraid of losing it]; ⁷ but made Himself of no reputation, taking the form of a bondservant, and coming in the likeness of men. ⁸ And being found in appearance as a man, He humbled Himself and became obedient to the point of death, even the death of the cross.*

God's Love Does Not Behave Rudely

Usually, when we think of someone being rude, we think of not considering the feelings of others, but the meaning of the word also includes the idea of behaving unbecomingly. Notice in the passage below that we are to imitate God as dear children. God walks in love and gave His Son for us. He does not behave rudely as is defined in verses three and four. He is the complete opposite.

> **Ephesians 5:3-4**
> *But fornication and all uncleanness or covetousness, let it not even be named among you, as is fitting for saints; ⁴ neither filthiness, nor foolish talking, nor coarse jesting, which are not fitting, but rather giving of thanks.*

God's Love Does Not Seek Its Own

Seeking is a good thing. We are to seek God with the purpose of getting an answer. Yet there is a negative type of seeking that is self-centered defined by Thayer this way:

> *To seek, i.e. require, demand; to crave, demand something from someone*

Love is not supposed to be demanding, yet consider all the self-seeking that goes on in a relationship such as marriage. Often in a marriage there is one person who is more persistent than the other who makes life a continual torture with his constant demands. Some people refuse to be satisfied.

On the contrary, God is working all things together for good for us. His focus is on our welfare. Every thought and action toward us is for our benefit. We need not worry that we might not think of Him every second. Rather, we should rejoice that He is always thinking of us—of us!

> ### Psalm 40:5
> *Many, O Lord my God,*
> *Are Your wonderful works*
> *Which You have done;*
> *And Your thoughts toward us*
> *Cannot be recounted to You in order;*
> *If I would declare and speak of them,*
> *They are more than can be numbered.*

God's Love is Not Provoked

While we expect fellow believers will not quickly become angry with us but will rather seek a resolution to conflict, this is not always the case. So, perhaps we view *God* as a hothead also. One little mistake on our part and some see God flying off the handle in rage toward us. Perhaps this is due to mixing Covenants or perhaps to not understanding what Jesus accomplished through His death and resurrection.[53]

Some Christians think God is upset with them for something as benign as having a dessert after dinner. Many live their whole day with the sense God is ticked-off at them for just about everything. Every negative thought they have about themselves they assume is God reprimanding them. If something goes wrong, they often conclude God is upset and getting back at them. No, our God is not vindictive. Instead of whacking us on the head, He lovingly teaches us.

This is very important to understand because sometimes we aren't perfect. When something happens as a result of our imperfections, we think God is spanking us and telling us how stupid we are.

Here's a common example. Let's say you are experiencing a health problem that restricts you from eating certain foods and you make the unwise choice of eating precisely what the doctor advised you not to eat. Suddenly, your body starts to react, and you have some undesirable physical symptom. Is this God saying, "I told you so," or isn't it your body simply responding to what you ate? If we think God is provoked and punishing us, how can we possibly receive forgiveness and help? Do we really think God leaves us on the road to die when we make mistakes? Certainly not!

Others worry they didn't spend every minute of the day doing *something* for the kingdom of God or they had a thought which wasn't exactly pure. They think He is upset because they spent money on a fancy coffee or on entertainment, especially in light of the poverty in the world. Because they are disgusted with themselves, they assume God is displeased with them also.

---

[53] If you are interested in more in-depth teachings on God's discipline, judgment and wrath, we recommend these teachings on our website which go into such topics and Ananias and Saphira. *https://graceandfaithministries.org/sgfteachings/judgement-and-discipline/*

Or we assume God is provoked against others because we are. We see Him as our partner in being infuriated at the injustice we observe. We might even think He is of a particular political party. I'd laugh right out loud at this point if there weren't so many Christians giving this impression.

Consider this, why would God expect *us* to not be easily provoked (or any of these characteristics of love we are considering), and not Himself be calm and loving toward us and toward others? If He did strike out against every injustice, our earth would surely melt.

Lamentations 3:22-23
Through the Lord's mercies we are not consumed,
Because His compassions fail not.
²³ They are new every morning;
Great is Your faithfulness.

Many believers today are also unaware of the following passage which reveals a completely different picture of God's attitude toward the sin of mankind under this New Covenant.

2 Corinthians 5:18-20
God... has given us the ministry of reconciliation,
*¹⁹ that is, that God was in Christ reconciling the world to Himself, **not imputing their trespasses to them**, and has committed to us the word of reconciliation. ²⁰ Now then, we are ambassadors for Christ, as though God were pleading through us: we implore you on Christ's behalf, **be reconciled to God**.*

God has given us the word of **reconciliation**.[54] What is that word? "God is not imputing your trespasses against you and is pleading with you to be reconciled to Him." Did you catch that? God is NOT holding the sins of the world against them. Jesus

---

[54] "Restoration to the divine favor." Strongs

died for the sins of the whole world, didn't He? While He was dying on the cross, He was reconciling God to man.

By no means does this imply all are automatically saved because there is one more essential aspect to reconciliation and we see it clearly above. God has reconciled Himself to the world, but the world must still reconcile itself to God. How? By believing in His Son.

> **John 3:17-20**
> *(Words in brackets are that of the author.)*
> *For God did not send His Son into the world to condemn the world, but that the world through Him might be saved. [He died to save the world by forgiving their sins.]* [18] *"He who believes in Him is not condemned; but he who does not believe is condemned already, because he has not believed in the name of the only begotten Son of God. [The reason men are condemned is not for the sins they have committed, but because of the sin of not believing in Him.]* [19] *And this is the condemnation, that the light has come into the world, and men loved darkness rather than light, because their deeds were evil. [Sin is an issue, but not because God is holding their sins against them, but because they love darkness rather than light.]* [20] *For everyone practicing evil hates the light and does not come to the light, lest his deeds should be exposed. [Jesus is the light.]*
> **John 8:24**
> *"Therefore I said to you that you will die in your sins;* **for if you do not believe that I am He**, *you will die in your sins." [The emphasis is on believing that Jesus is who He claims to be—God.]*

Jesus didn't die to condemn the world for their sins. He came to forgive them for their sins. When He died, all sin was dealt with leaving us with this glorious ministry of reconciliation: God is not holding our sins against us. Because our sins have been forgiven, the only sin from which mankind must now turn away in order to be reconciled to Him is that of not believing in Him. Please continue reading. This is precisely why the gospel is "good" news—God is not angry with us. He is not holding our sins against us. He has reconciled Himself to us. Now, we must be reconciled to Him.

God knows that when we believe in Him, we will become new creations who are forevermore free from the dominion of sin (Rom. 6:14). We will *want* to please Him because our hearts will cry out, "Abba, Father!" He is not now our personal sin-hound sniffing out every flaw. No! He is now convincing us we are His righteousness (Jn. 16:9-10). Instead of seeing Him at your heels barking and biting each time you make a mistake in word or thought or deed, start seeing Him as He is, in your heart assuring you that you are *right* with Him, that your sins are forgiven, that He is on your side, and that He is working in you to bring about His desire for your life.

God's Love Thinks No Evil

This is a difficult one for most human beings, even for some Christians. We tend to read evil motivations into the actions of others even when there is no human way possible to know another's heart. Sometimes, we ourselves might have unjust motives for what we do, so we often project our ideas on others.

This aspect of love, that of not thinking evil of others almost doesn't apply to God's love for us for He knows everyone's every thought. He doesn't need the ability to assume the worst or best about anyone for He is all-knowing.

One of the most peaceful aspects of our relationship with God is knowing that He knows all. We don't need to justify or excuse ourselves or exalt ourselves before Him. He knows, so we can simply be open and honest with Him. What rest!

God's Love Does Not Rejoice in Iniquity

To think that God would rejoice in evil is absurd, yet some people still think God brings about evil to produce good in our lives. The opposite is more where our focus should be when speaking of God's love.

God's Love Rejoices in the Truth

The opposite of rejoicing in iniquity is rejoicing in the truth. When justice is served, when rights are wronged, when we begin to see the truth of His love for us, God rejoices. He takes no pleasure in death or affliction, rather He rejoices when truth and life prevail.

God's Love Bears All Things

When thinking of "bearing" something, I think of enduring under pressure, but the Greek definition of the word delights my heart for it is much more than that.[55]

1) deck, thatch, to cover
a) to protect or keep by covering, to preserve
2) to cover over with silence
a) to keep secret
b) to hide, conceal
1) of the errors and faults of others
3) by covering to keep off something which threatens, to bear up against, hold out against, and so endure, bear, forbear

We don't often think of God's love this way—as covering and protecting us, keeping our secrets, covering our errors and faults. Some even think God will go out of His way to *expose* our every thought and that He has given them the ministry of

---

[55] Thayer

telling everyone about the flaws of others. God is not like this. He covers our sins.

Remember the story of Noah, who after the flood, planted a vineyard, made wine from the grapes, and then got drunk and uncovered himself in his tent. His youngest son delighted in telling his two brothers about what was going on, but they took a blanket and walked backward into the tent to cover their father's nakedness. This accurately reflects God's heart.

1 Peter 4:8
And above all things have fervent love for one another, for "love will cover a multitude of sins."

God's Love Believes All Things

Faith does not stand alone. There is always an object of our faith, either in something or someone. Love believes all things, but that doesn't mean we believe lies or put our trust in those who are not trustworthy. Of course, not. To "believe all things" is to believe in God's good character. It is to believe He will do as He has promised. It is to "believe He rewards those who seek Him."

How might we view this in terms of God as a faith being? Obviously, there is no higher power than He, so He does not need to put His faith in anyone. Yet He is abounding in faith—faith in Himself. He spoke, and the universes were created. Paul described it this way. "He gives life to the dead and calls those things which do not exist as though they did," (Rom. 4:17). Does God doubt Himself? Certainly not.

When preparing something for someone to eat, I have total confidence that the person will love it because I trust in my skills. Perhaps you are creating a piece of artwork with total faith it will come out just as you planned. As a teacher or parent you rely on your teaching/parenting methods to develop your student or child.

God has even more confidence in what He has done. He made us new creations and He has faith in the power He placed in us to totally transform us. He sets His word in motion with full faith it will accomplish what He sends it out to do (Isa. 55:11).

> ### Romans 8:11
> *But if the Spirit of Him who raised Jesus from the dead dwells in you, He who raised Christ from the dead will also give life to your mortal bodies through His Spirit who dwells in you.*

God's Love Hopes All Things

Earlier in the book, "hope" was defined as "a supremely joyful confident expectation of good," and this is our God. He is the God of hope. He has a joyful and confident expectation of good in our lives because He both works in us and for us for our good.

> ### Romans 15:13
> *Now may the God of hope fill you with all joy and peace in believing, that you may abound in hope by the power of the Holy Spirit.*

We can be insecure at times—uneasy about the future, less than confident about our abilities, and bent down low by storms that come into our lives. If we put our hope in ourselves, we will continue to struggle. If we put our hope in the God of hope, we find strength.

Taking off in a flight when it is raining outside can be a bit unsettling, but in minutes you are above the storm. Down below people are taking out umbrellas, running for shelter, and delaying outdoor activities, but you are soaring above it all with nothing but blue skies above. God's perspective on the troubles we encounter is very different from ours. He sees the whole picture. Instead of fear and dread, God joyfully antici-pates the good He is sending and our joy in receiving it.

God's Love Endures All Things

We know what it means to endure. A summary of Thayer's definition is to remain, to tarry behind, abide, not recede or flee, to hold fast to one's faith in Christ, to bear bravely and calmly. Every person on earth faces hard times. What sets one person apart from the other is one's willingness to endure instead of giving up.

Many things in life require endurance. Consider the first-time mother who has slept uncomfortably for many nights during pregnancy, gone through the pain of childbirth and then returns home to lingering pain, a baby needing constant care, and more sleepless nights. Love empowers her to endure with almost no reward. Why does she endure? Love.

This transition from woman to mother can be very difficult. Gradually, patience grows as she realizes that any sacrifice she gives imparts life and love to her child. Endurance grows to such a degree that the thought of doing it all over again begins to sound like a wonderful idea.

As a parent, God's endurance is constantly put to the test. Imagine what He sees on a day to day basis. We live in a world that is becoming more and more corrupt. Even those who believe in Jesus, His beloved children, often put Him to the test, believing in the lies of the enemy instead of the Promises of their Father. He endures. He patiently teaches us.

When we are exasperated with ourselves, He remains calm. He promised He would never ever leave us, and He will not. He won't abandon us when times get hard. He will encourage us and persevere with us always.

God's Love Never Fails

The literal meaning of the word "never" here is "not ever at any time." Don't you love that? Love, God's love, never fails, but most of us have witnessed human love failing us repeatedly. God's love for us will not at any time ever fail us because "God IS love." It is His very heart and character. May we never compare His ability to love with ours. We fail at times. He

273

never does. He loves us more than we will ever be able to comprehend.

God endures with patience and serenity.
God is kind and thoughtful,
and He is not jealous or envious;
God does not brag, and He is not proud or arrogant.
⁵ He is not rude; He is not self-seeking.
He is not provoked [nor overly sensitive and easily angered];
God does not take into account a wrong endured.
⁶ He does not rejoice at injustice.
but rejoices with the truth [when right and truth prevail].
⁷ God bears all things [regardless of what comes],
believes all things [looking for the best in each one],
hopes all things [remaining steadfast during difficult times],
endures all things [without weakening].
⁸ God's love never fails [it never fades nor ends].

1 Corinthians 13:4-8 AMP[56]

Continuing the Journey

1. Consider 1 Corinthians 13:4-8 again. What stands out to you about God's love that perhaps you hadn't noticed before?

2. How does knowing we are loved by God these ways influence the way we relate to others?

---

[56] *"Love" has been replaced with "God."*

Chapter 33

OUR FIRST LOVE

Revelation 2:4
Nevertheless I have this against you, that you have left your first love.

As young adults, this verse was menacing to us. God forbid we would lose our first love! When we'd hear sermons about this, especially when mixed with the thought of being lukewarm, we would examine our lives carefully to affirm that our love for God was sure and our dedication unwavering. This perception of these verses fit perfectly with our ever-increasing list of "spiritual disciplines" and our desire to demonstrate our love for God by doing them.

It's worthy of mention (even though it doesn't perfectly fit in with this topic) that not only was our diligence directed toward pleasing God, but we desired with all of our hearts to be used by God in "mighty" ways in ministry (Daniel 11:32), and we were constantly taught God would use us in proportion to how diligently we sought Him which was accomplished through dedication to completing "the list" and working exhaustively and passionately for Him in full-time ministry.

Never mind that by anyone's evaluation, we *were* doing what we'd been told to do, and yet the promised revival through us wasn't happening. "Remain faithful to the end," we were encouraged. Results weren't the point. It was our "faithfulness" that mattered most to God. Even though our discipline

and diligence were steadfast, we were not seeing the promised "move of God."

When we were freed from these invented laws, the above
verse finally came to light in its context. Let's take another look.

> **Revelation 2:1-5**
> *To the angel of the church of Ephesus write,*
> *These things says He who holds the seven*
> *stars in His right hand, who walks in the midst*
> *of the seven golden lampstands: ² "I know*
> *your works, your labor, your patience, and that*
> *you cannot bear those who are evil. And you*
> *have tested those who say they are apostles*
> *and are not, and have found them liars; ³ and*
> *you have persevered and have patience, and*
> *have labored for My name's sake and have*
> *not become weary. ⁴ Nevertheless I have this*
> *against you, that you have left your first love.*
> *⁵ Remember therefore from where you have*
> *fallen; repent and do the first works, or else*
> *I will come to you quickly and remove your*
> *lampstand from its place—unless you repent."*

If remembering their first love meant they needed to be more
diligent, there would be no reason to correct the Ephesians.
In fact, they are commended for their persistence. They had
good works. They labored in the gospel. They were patient in
suffering and persecutions. They did not tolerate false apostles
and exposed them as liars. They labored with long suffering
for His' sake without growing weary in doing good.

They had taken Paul's advice to them as he departed.

> **Ephesians 20:28-32**
> *"Therefore take heed to yourselves and to all the*
> *flock, among which the Holy Spirit has made*
> *you overseers, to shepherd the church of God*
> *which He purchased with His own blood. ²⁹ For*
> *I know this, that after my departure savage*

wolves will come in among you, not sparing the flock. ³⁰ Also from among yourselves men will rise up, speaking perverse things, to draw away the disciples after themselves. ³¹ Therefore watch and remember that for three years I did not cease to warn everyone night and day with tears.

³² "So now, brethren, I commend you to God and to the word of His grace, which is able to build you up and give you an inheritance among all those who are sanctified."

So, leaving one's first love could not refer to a lack of diligence as we formerly believed. Truly, the Ephesians were diligent, even to the point of making sure the wolves among them were exposed and rejected. Even so, Paul also wrote this to the Ephesians.

Ephesians 3:15-19

*For this reason I bow my knees to the Father of our Lord Jesus Christ, ¹⁵ from whom the whole family in heaven and earth is named, ¹⁶ that He would grant you, according to the riches of His glory, to be strengthened with might through His Spirit in the inner man, ¹⁷ that Christ may dwell in your hearts through faith; that you, **being rooted and grounded in love, ¹⁸ may be able to comprehend with all the saints what is the width and length and depth and height— ¹⁹ to know the love of Christ which passes knowledge; that you may be filled with all the fullness of God.***

Surely this is a prayer for us all, but perhaps Paul prayed this specifically for the Ephesians because he perceived they *needed* to be rooted and grounded in the love of Christ. Perhaps in their zeal to serve the Lord, they lost track of the most important aspect of the Christian life—our loving relationship with God.

What has happened to Christians throughout the centuries is also something that can happen to us. We experienced firsthand this diminishing of the importance of knowing we are loved by God. We loved God so much we were motivated to please Him and work diligently for Him (there is nothing wrong with that), but in the process, we lost our first love of His love for *us* while we were focusing mostly on proving our love for *Him*. Instead of acknowledging and believing in His love for us—that love we knew the hour we "first believed," we sought through our works to love God with all our being.

To be rooted and grounded in love is likely two things at the same time. First, we must be confident He loves us. The second thing is we love fellow believers as Jesus loved us. A tree that is rooted and grounded often has a deeper root system than the size of the tree itself. However, a young tree whose roots are not grounded or an old tree whose roots never went deep enough will blow over in the first major storm.

One who knows he is loved by God will not waiver in that belief when hard times happen. Those who are not firmly planted in God's love for them will faint when the wind and waves try to overcome them, sometimes even blaming God for their circumstances instead of reaching out for His love and help through them.

God's desire for us is to be rooted and grounded deeply in His love for us. He wants our knowledge of His love to increase and for us to be firmly convinced of it. He wants us to believe in His love in good times and bad. We need not look far for evidence.

John 3:16 HCSB
For God loved the world in this way: He gave His One and Only Son, so that everyone who believes in Him will not perish but have eternal life.

Jesus suffered and died because He loved us. This one demonstration of love is all we need to be persuaded of His love for us. He rescued us from darkness and death and set us in the kingdom of light and life.

1 John 4:9
In this the love of God was manifested toward us, that God has sent His only begotten Son into the world, that we might live through Him.

Yet the church continues to emphasize our love toward God instead of His love for us.

A few years ago, I went to a Christian bookstore to find a discipleship book for new believers. Flipping the pages of several booklets broke my heart. There was no information about how much they were loved by God and no encouragement to love the saints. There were no lessons on our total forgiveness or our righteousness by faith and not a word about living by grace through faith.

What I found for the most part were the beginnings of that list I've mentioned so many times. "Now that you are a Christian, you will need to find a church and attend regularly. Get a good Bible and read it daily. Pray every day. Get involved in your local church in some way. Find someone who's been a believer longer than you and ask him to be your mentor." How very sad it is that this indoctrination begins almost at Day 1 of a new believer's life.

In fact, not only new believers, but we all are more likely to hear sermons about how we must live and what God expects of us than to ever be reminded of God's great love *for* us. Can you remember hearing such a sermon focusing only on God's love for us without "balancing" the teaching with what *we* are supposed to do to merit or reciprocate His love?

It is time for the church to examine our perspectives. We need to get our eyes on Jesus so we are free to enjoy the love of God.

In this is love,
not that we loved God,
e **but that He loved us** f
and sent His Son to be the propitiation for our sins.

1 John 4:10

Continuing the Journey

1. Do you remember a time when your emphasis was on you loving God rather than on God loving you? Describe that time of your life.

2. What might a believer experience as he returns to his first love—God's love for him?

Chapter 34

LOVE IN ACTION

---

*W*hile 1 Corinthians 13:4-8 is rightfully considered the quintessential illustration of love, we have many more manifestations of His love to explore, because, though it is true God gave us all things pertaining to life and godliness, Paul prayed for the Ephesians to know the height and depth and length and width of God's love for them—which, he adds, **surpasses** knowledge. So, while we already have all things pertaining to life and godliness, we are encouraged to deepen our understanding when it comes to His love for us. Since His love is infinite, our discovery is forever. Think of that! For all eternity, we will be able to explore His great love.

This is not to say we are to seek to "feel" His love more (though we all treasure those moments), but rather we are encouraged "to *know* the love of Christ which passes knowledge; that we may be filled with all the fullness of God" (Eph. 3:19).

You see, real love does not exist in the isolation of sentiment. Just as faith is demonstrated in some type of action, be it as simple as a spoken word such as confessing Jesus is the Lord or taking steps of faith as we understand the will of God in our lives, so love takes shape in demonstration—actions. Thus, while we need not seek to be "closer" to God or become increasingly righteous and holy, for example, we *are* invited to be rooted and grounded in His great love for us.

Our individualized journeys toward rediscovering our first love—God's love for us, will likely be shaped by the reasons we strayed from it in the first place. As children following the crumbs we left behind to find our way home, we will need to retrace our walk with God reexamining everything we've ever been taught about what it means to be a Christian and how that encouraged or discouraged us from knowing and believing we are loved by Him. This will take time and courage.

Others will need to conscientiously allow God to shed light on the negative things they experienced that put in doubt God's character and His promised love. They will need healing from wrongs done to them, and His grace to forgive so they may live truly free from the effects of misdeeds committed against them.

What each of us must understand is that even though we may immediately return to the knowledge and faith of our first love—that of knowing we are unconditionally loved by our God, it may take years for God to fully weed out the damage done by false teachings and loathsome experiences. That's why it's a journey. It's a wonderful voyage full of discovery and freedom, but also one that challenges our former opinions and thus requires us to stay open to the workings of the Holy Spirit in our hearts. Don't be afraid, and don't rush the process. He heals as He reveals.

Let me also address specifically those of you who failed to love and those who taught inaccurately about the importance of God's love. You are not excluded from this circle of caring. God has forgiven you also and He reaches out to you with great love. As you study the Bible, you will repeatedly see that God extends mercy and grace to all.

Abraham lied; Jacob was a deceiver; Rahab was a prostitute; David was a murderer and adulterer; Paul the apostle consented to the killing and imprisoning of Christians. Yet God expressed His compassion to them all, even bringing them to a place of being used for His glory.

As you seek forgiveness from those you harmed, please know that even though those you hurt in the past may choose to not forgive you, God does.

It's also important to keep in mind that God's love for *us* does not have a period at the end of the sentence. It is in His heart's desire that we will love each other as He has loved us.

> **John 15:9-13**
> *"As the Father loved Me, I also have loved you; abide in My love. ¹⁰ If you keep My commandments, you will abide in My love, just as I have kept My Father's commandments and abide in His love.*
> *¹¹ "These things I have spoken to you, that My joy may remain in you, and that your joy may be full.¹² This is My commandment, that you love one another as I have loved you. ¹³ Greater love has no one than this, than to lay down one's life for his friends."*

So, be encouraged as you examine these expressions of God's love for you, and keep in mind how God might use you to share this same quality of love with others, especially within the body of Christ, for as Jesus said, "As you have done these things to the least of these my brethren, you have done them unto me."[57]

God's love is like a beautiful gem with multiple facets that speak to our every need. Take your time with this chapter. Each subtitle is packed with truths we need to walk confidently in His love.

God of Love

God is love. Just that one fact changes us forever. We need to keep it foremost in our thoughts. God not only is love, He is the God of love. Thus, love is not only the core of who He is, love is what He does. We must challenge and vanquish all false narratives out there about who He is and what He

---

[57] Since the focus of this book is God's love for us, I will leave the applications of our love for each other to the reader.

does—anything that accuses Him of motives and actions that do not reflect His love.

> ### 2 Corinthians 13:11
> *Finally, brethren, farewell. Become complete. Be of good comfort, be of one mind, live in peace; and the **God of love** and peace will be with you.*

God's Love Appears

> ### Titus 3:4
> *But when the kindness and the love of God our Savior toward man appeared…*

We know God's love appeared to mankind through the life, death, and resurrection of Jesus. How thankful we are for these demonstrations of love toward us. Consider this also—God's love appears in our lives today. When we face troubles, His love shows up to rescue us. When we are falsely accused, His love comforts. His love manifests itself to us in the form of answered prayer and the kindness shown to us by others. His love shows itself when we are shown undeserved grace by those we offended. Keep your eyes open. His love is constantly appearing.

God's Love Forgives

God's love forgives us. Words cannot express the peace of knowing we were and are and always will be forgiven. God forgives us for **everything**, especially all the things for which we tend not to forgive ourselves such as an imperfect thought, an unkind word, being self-centered, not being the sharpest tack in the drawer, not being the model of perfection, not finishing our to-do list, eating two pieces of pizza instead of one, not being as successful as we thought we would be by now, feeling depressed when we should be rejoicing, experiencing fear when we should be believing in Him, and the list goes on.

For all the areas where we think we are not good enough, God forgives. He is absolutely not holding our weaknesses against us at any time, rather He is working in us and through us 24/7/365 to make us who He wants us to be and to do what He's called us to do. Thus, we can rest in the love of His forgiveness.

God's Love Heals

Many Christians find it difficult to believe that God will heal them because they combine "justice" with "forgiveness." They believe God can only heal them or help them if their situation is not their doing, but they don't believe He will help them if they caused the problem.

Let's be honest. While, of course, things happen to us that are no fault of our own, many of the difficulties and health problems we face are ones in which we bear at least partial responsibility.

Many do not manage their finances well and find themselves backed up in debt they cannot pay. Others smoked tobacco, spent too much time in the sun, ate poorly, took drugs, didn't wear protective gear as needed, and now they are "reaping what they have sown." Relationships among family and friends are strained because they were unkind and self-centered or behaved inappropriately. Does God ignore these beloved ones?

We have several sayings in the U.S.A. which express the sentiment that if you do something that creates a problem, that problem is yours to solve. We say, "You made your bed. Now lie in it," or "If you do the crime, then you do the time," or "You get what you pay for." These sayings are true, but in God's economy, "Mercy triumphs over judgment," (Js. 2:13), and "Love covers a multitude of sins," (1 Pet. 4:8). While many sayings and even misappropriated Scripture make perfect sense, if they are based only on us getting what we deserve and do not include the mercy of God, then they are not correct.

Romans 3:23
*For the wages of sin is death, **but** the gift of
God is eternal life in Christ Jesus our Lord.*

Yes, the wages of sin is death, BUT God freely gives us
eternal life. The concept of us *deserving* salvation is completely out of place. Anyone suggesting any other way to be
saved other than faith, is considered a heretic.

Then why do we go on thinking that healing and help from
God are something we work to deserve and receive? Does
He heal and help because we've been good boys and girls,
or are not these things also given and received by grace
through faith? Indeed, forgiveness, healing, help, and whatever we receive from God is a *gift*. Please allow this to sink
into your heart.

Galatians 3:5
*Therefore He who supplies the Spirit to you
and works miracles among you, **does He do
it by the works of the law**, or by the hearing
of faith?*

God doesn't do any miracle because we follow the law
or are extraordinarily diligent. He does miracles because He
extended the free gift of them, and we believe. When we
understand that we are forgiven, it is much easier to believe
that His love reaches out to us to heal. This includes healing of
the spirit, soul, and body. God is willing to repair the damage
done to us and clean up the messes we have made.

Perhaps you have a lifetime of making the wrong financial
choices. God isn't abandoning you to your own works. He's
not ashamed of you. No! He is working in you to make wiser
choices and will provide for you so that you no longer live in
poverty or in debt. He will help you find additional employment
so you can finally be free.

We need to see that the God who freely saves, freely helps
us. This is very important because the enemy will accuse us
and shame us and try to get our eyes on our own failures and

tell us we can't expect God to help us after we messed up. That is not true. He will help us. Not only will He help us clean up the mess we've made, He will change us from the inside out, so we will be able to avoid the same mistakes in the future. Oh, how wonderful is our God's love for us.

> ### Romans 8:32
> *He who did not spare His own Son, but delivered Him up for us all, how shall He not with Him also **freely** give us **all** things?*

God's Love Gives Life

> ### 1 John 4:9
> *In this the **love of God** was manifested toward us, that God has sent His only begotten Son into the world, that we might **live** through Him.*

One of the manifestations of God's love toward us is that we might have life, yet it is likely that you've heard more sermons about "dying to self" than living this life in Him.

Jesus said, "The enemy comes to steal, to kill, and destroy. I have come that you may have life and have it to the fullest." If there is stealing, killing, or destruction going on in your life, that is NOT from God. His love reaches out to give us LIFE—abundant life!

How many of us walk around half dead simply going through the motions in life? Yes, we love God and are learning more about His love for us, but we are afraid of being too happy and too alive, for fear that it will all come crashing down on us one day.

God's love was given to us that we might LIVE through Him. Why do we subdue that joy of His life living through us instead of celebrating it? Think about it, when was the last time you rejoiced about the everlasting life you have?

Maybe it's because we've seen that people who are "too" happy in Jesus are often ostracized within the church. Perhaps it's because our sermons focus more on what we need to *do*

287

for Jesus rather than what Jesus did/does for us. Think about it. Are you allowing the love of God to *live* through you?

This is a topic deserving of its own book. If you'd like, look up the words "live" and "life" in a concordance or search engine remembering that this is an expression of God's love for us. You will be amazed by how often the Bible speaks of us having life!

> **John 4:14**
> *Whoever drinks of the water that I shall give him will never thirst. But the water that I shall give him will become in him a **fountain of water springing up into everlasting life**."*
> **John 7:38**
> *He who believes in Me, as the Scripture has said, out of his heart will **flow rivers of living water**."*

God's Love Highly Favors

> **Ephesians 1:3-6**
> *Blessed be the God and Father of our Lord Jesus Christ, who has blessed us with every spiritual blessing in the heavenly places in Christ, ⁴ just as He chose us in Him before the foundation of the world, that we should be holy and without blame before Him in love, ⁵ having predestined us to adoption as sons by Jesus Christ to Himself, according to the good pleasure of His will, ⁶ to the praise of the glory of His grace, by which He made us accepted in the Beloved.*

Depending on the version of the Bible you are reading, the English word "accept" and its variations appear nearly 100 times in the Old and New Testaments, but the original word in the Hebrew or Greek is not always the same. The meanings vary from tolerating something or receiving something in a positive sense to the idea of being approved and well-pleasing.

The word translated "accepted" in verse six above, however, is only used twice in Scripture and carries a different meaning than one might expect given the word "accepted" as we commonly think of it. The word is **charitoō** which comes from **charis** (grace). **Charitoō** means, "to grace, that is, endue with special honor: - make accepted, be highly favored."[58] The meaning of **charitoō** translated in the other passage brings forth this definition more straightforwardly.

> ### Luke 1:26-28
> *Now in the sixth month the angel Gabriel was sent by God to a city of Galilee named Nazareth, 27 to a virgin betrothed to a man whose name was Joseph, of the house of David. The virgin's name was Mary. 28 And having come in, the angel said to her, "Rejoice, **highly favored one**, the Lord is with you; blessed are you among women!"*

God endued Mary with the special honor of being the mother of the Messiah. There is no indication Mary merited this grace in any way, except that her lineage was what it needed to be, and yet she was *highly* favored of God. This changes our perception from being simply *"accepted* in the Beloved" (which is glorious enough) to that of being endued/graced with special honor, of being made acceptable and highly favored in God's beloved Son. For me, that takes a second read-through.

❧ We are highly favored in the Beloved. ❧

God's Love Accepts

It is important for us to learn that God accepts us. Some do not doubt God loves them, but when it comes to being

---

[58] Strong's

accepted by God, that is another matter. Many went through all the "spiritual" exercises they were told would make them a successful Christian or minister, only to be faced with the fact their efforts produced few results. It's easy to begin thinking God is disappointed with them.

Yet as we look at Hebrews 11 we see God is not praising their works, but rather their faith that brought about the good works. Faith is what pleases God. He is not counting up all of our "success" in life and ministry (as we humans tend to do). He is seeing our faith. We are accepted by Him because we put our faith in Jesus.

Whatever we end up doing in God's kingdom is really God's business. We express our willingness, but He is the one who calls. Whatever He calls us to do, be it a career, parenting, or ministry, let us do it by faith. One might be more "successful" in the eyes of others and another go unnoticed, but it doesn't matter. Our God accepts us all. May His will be done in all our lives. Amen. He does the calling. We simply respond by faith.

> **Romans 9:16**
> *So then it is not of him who wills, nor of him who runs, but of God who shows mercy.*

God's Love Gives

There was a time in our life when we had very little money. We fed our family, paid our bills, gave in the offering plate, and that was about all we could do. Many people during that time were very kind and generous with us, and it blessed our hearts. Way back then we longed for a day when *we* could be on the giving side of the equation. Jesus said, "It is more blessed to give than receive," and who can disagree with that? Now that we have something to share, it is a total blessing to give to this one and that, to minister to our children, and grandchildren, and friends. Giving is such a cheerful endeavor.

God loves giving to His children. So many passages encourage us to ask and receive. God wants to bring us joy by answering our prayers even though Paul wrote that He gave us "all things pertaining to life and godliness." Some might say that since we have been given all, we need not ask for more— simply enjoy what He has given. Yet Paul also wrote that He is "able to do exceedingly abundantly above all that we can ask or think," and, "He rewards those who seek Him."

As mentioned earlier, it is more common to hear a sermon about what God expects of us than to be reminded of all He's given and will give. In fact, many people go to church on Sunday to discover more about what God expects of them rather than going to hear of what He wants to give them. Focusing on what God does for us is sometimes seen as a self-centered Christianity, but it's actually quite the opposite. It is a Jesus-centered perspective. It *does* matter what we do in this life, but what we do is based upon what He has already done.

We need to put the cart behind the horse and jump inside. Jesus is powering this wagon. We are going along for the ride. It is because He loved us and died for us that we live. It is because He was wounded that we are healed. It was because He told us to speak to mountains that they move. It is because He brought us to Himself that we fellowship with Him. We give because He gave. He gave and He gives because He loves.

God's Love Cares

God is not impassive toward us. We are in His thoughts continually and His intentions toward us are good. He deeply cares about what we are going through and reaches out to help us when we call on His name.

Hebrews 4:15-16
For we do not have a High Priest who cannot sympathize with our weaknesses, but was in all points tempted as we are, yet without sin. 16 Let us therefore come boldly to the throne of grace, that we may obtain mercy and find grace to help in time of need.

We can come before God in confidence because His heart is tender toward us. He won't ignore us or make light of our prayers. He lived on this earth and knows what it's like. We will find mercy and grace to help us in our time of need. When this old world is beating us down, He doesn't watch us to see what we will do. Instead, He immediately begins to work for good anything done against us. He partners with us in our grief.

Romans 8:26
Likewise the Spirit also helps in our weaknesses. For we do not know what we should pray for as we ought, but the Spirit Himself makes intercession for us with groanings which cannot be uttered.

God's Love Comforts

2 Corinthians 1:3-4
Blessed be the God and Father of our Lord Jesus Christ, the Father of mercies and God of all comfort, ⁴ who comforts us in all our tribulation, that we may be able to comfort those who are in any trouble, with the comfort with which we ourselves are comforted by God.

Life gets hard sometimes. People we love pass away. Disappointments come. Those we love sometimes betray and reject us. Youth fades. Spouses leave. Sickness challenges. Finances fall through. Often several of these things happen at once. When these things happen, it feels as if our hearts cannot endure the grief.

How thankful I am for the comfort of God. When my mother passed away, my very best friend was lost. How deeply her passing broke my heart. Although people tried to encourage me, there was a pain within me that was more profound than anyone could reach. I sunk into deep sadness from which only He could rescue me. It took every ounce of energy to continue being mom and wife in a way that wouldn't bring them down with me while agonizing in pain every minute of each day.

Thankfully, God's love comforted me. The God of all comfort reached down and brought me through what seemed impossible to endure. Every time I wanted to talk to her and couldn't, His love reached out to me. As family events came up that she would not be able to attend, He comforted me. When I went through seasons of life when I needed her wise counsel to guide me, God guided me. Even now, when I see my friends ministering to their aging parents and realize that my mom would also be in her nineties and perhaps in my care, God reaches out to me in love. He will help you also. Be sure of it. He is faithful.

> *Now, my mother and I*
> *Became the dearest friends*
> *I always knew she loved me*
> *From her heart,*
> *But twenty years before I thought she would*
> *She went to be with You*
> *Leaving behind a broken heart.*
>
> *But Father, You've been the Daddy*
> *Daddy refused to be.*
> *Jesus, you're the brother*
> *Daddy took away from me, and*
> *Holy Spirit You're the Comforter*
> *That Mommy always was.*
> *God, You filled the emptiness in me.*
> *God, You are my family.*[59]

God comforts us so deeply and entirely that we are able to sing a new song to Him—to praise Him once again.

---

[59] "God, You Are My Family", part of a song by C. D. Hildebrand, circa 1990

Psalm 30:11-12

You have turned for me my mourning into dancing;
You have put off my sackcloth and clothed me with gladness,
12 To the end that my glory may sing praise to You and not be silent.
O Lord my God, I will give thanks to You forever.

God's Love is Present

God's love is with us. It was with us when He came as Emmanuel and was demonstrated by His every word and deed as He lived among us. He proved His great love to us when He gave Himself in death to give us life. He is present with us now.

2 Corinthians 13:14

The grace of the Lord Jesus Christ, and the love of God, and the communion of the Holy Spirit be with you all.

Nothing can separate us from God's love for us. Nothing— not the enemy who lies, nor the persecutions we face, nor the troubles that come our way, not even our own sin.

Romans 8:38-39

For I am persuaded that neither death nor life, nor angels nor principalities nor powers, nor things present nor things to come, 39 nor height nor depth, nor any other created thing, shall be able to separate us from the love of God which is in Christ Jesus our Lord.

When others fail, even those who are the closest to us, His love will still remain.

Psalm 27:10
When my father and my mother forsake me,
Then the Lord will take care of me.
Psalm 91:15
He shall call upon Me, and I will answer him;
I will be with him in trouble;
I will deliver him and honor him.

God's Love Corrects

One of the powerful evidences we have that we are loved as children by God is the fact that He teaches and corrects us. Some of us cringe at the thought of being disciplined by God because we unnecessarily fear His wrath instead of seeing Him as a loving Father.

Though we certainly do not enjoy correction, we should be thankful for it and the love behind it. We can be going about our lives and subtly be making choices that do not line up with God's truth, when suddenly, it seems, God gently does not allow us to feel peace about where we are heading. As we listen, His grace teaches us, His Spirit leads us, and we eventually yield to His will. The process can be difficult, but the result is peace.

Blessed be the God and Father of our Lord Jesus Christ, who has blessed us with every spiritual blessing in the heavenly places in Christ, 4 just as He chose us in Him before the foundation of the world, that we would be holy and blameless before Him. **In love**[5] *He predestined us to adoption as sons through Jesus Christ to Himself, according to the kind intention of His will, 6 to the praise of the glory of His grace, which He freely bestowed on us in the Beloved. 7 In Him we have redemption through His blood, the forgiveness of our trespasses, according to the riches of His grace 8 which He* **lavished** *on us.*

Ephesians 1:3-8

Continuing the Journey

1. Reflect on some of the examples of God's love listed above. Which stand out to you in a personal way?

2. It is my sincerest endeavor when writing to be thorough but also concise. Yet how does one stop singing the praises of the love of God? It just isn't possible. Even after covering "everything," something else comes to mind. So, let me give you a list of other ways the love of God expresses itself to us for you to consider. Discuss or record your responses. Can you think of others?

    - *God's love says, "Yes."*
    - *God's love takes action.*
    - *God's love respects.*
    - *God's love lifts up.*
    - *God's love fellowships with us.*
    - *God's love provides.*
    - *God's love protects.*
    - *God's love promises.*
    - *God's love predicts.*
    - *God's love prepares.*
    - *God's love praises.*
    - *God's love listens.*

3. It's important to keep in mind when we are out in public that behind each face is a story. During the course of one day, you might be standing next to someone who just lost a family member or friend. Or the cashier who was not as patient as he should have been, just found out his wife wants a divorce. The guy who was going too fast on the freeway might have just lost his job. Children we meet might not be living in a loving environment, and just one kind word from us can make such a difference. As

parents and teachers we must always keep this in mind. Let us make it our goal to never humiliate a child in any way, but to show kindness to all. How might we incorporate this awareness in our day to day living?

Chapter 35

KNOW AND BELIEVE

Galatians 2:20
*I have been crucified with Christ; it is no longer I who live, but Christ lives in me; and the life which I now live in the flesh I live by faith in the Son of God, **who loved me and gave Himself for me.***

*T*he very core of the message of the gospel is that Jesus *loved* us and *gave* Himself for us. When we understand and believe this one simple truth, it is enough to last a lifetime. No matter what comes our way, we can remember His love and receive His grace.

Galatians 2:21
*I do not set aside the **grace of God**; for if **righteousness** comes through the law, then Christ **died** in vain."*

We must acknowledge that the message of the above verse is directly connected to the one that precedes it. We were made righteous (free from guilt or sin, justified)[60] by faith in Jesus who "loved us and gave Himself for us." It was His love that sent Him to the cross, and that love had a purpose—to

---

[60] Merriam-Webster Dictionary

make us righteous, and righteousness is a gift. When we believed in Jesus we received abundance of grace and the gift of righteousness.

> **Romans 5:17**
> *For if by the one man's offense death reigned through the one, much more those who receive abundance of grace and of the **gift of righteousness** will reign in life through the One, Jesus Christ.*

Again, Jesus gave His life because He loved us. When He died, He made us His very righteousness by forgiving our sins and canceling out the law that was contrary to us so we could never be made unrighteous again.[61]

> **Colossians 2:13-14**
> *And you, being **dead** in your trespasses and the uncircumcision of your flesh, He has made **alive** together with Him, having **forgiven** you all trespasses, [14] having **wiped out** the handwriting of requirements that was against us, which was contrary to us. And He has taken it out of the way, having nailed it to the cross.*

These were gifts to us by His grace. We must associate the grace of God with the love of God that sent His only Son to die in our place so that we would become His righteousness. We are not only righteous; we are the righteousness of God.

> **2 Corinthians 5:21**
> *For He made Him who knew no sin to be a sin-offering for us, so that we might become the righteousness of God.*

---

[61] Among MANY other things

Certainly it is equally significant that Paul writes in Galatians 2:20, "and the **life** which I now **live** in the flesh I **live** by **faith** in the Son of God." We have eternal life, abundant life, overflowing life. This life we live while in our human bodies is lived by *faith* in Jesus not by following laws. Think about this, please. We don't **live** by following laws because the law doesn't give life. We live this life by believing in Him.

> **Galatians 3:21-22**
> For **if** there had been a law given which **could** have given life, truly **righteousness would** have been by the law. ²² **But** the Scripture has confined all under sin, that the promise (of righteousness) by **faith** in Jesus Christ might be **given** to those who **believe**.

We must take heed **not to set aside this glorious grace**, this life, that has been gifted to us because of His unfathomable **love.** We are making His sacrifice of no value when we equate our righteousness with how carefully we are following the law, be it the Ten Commandments or the hundreds of invented laws of Christianity—we are setting aside His love as insignificant.

ॐ **Nothing, absolutely nothing makes us right with God beyond what Jesus accomplished at the cross.** ॐ

When we know how deeply we are loved by God, we will want nothing more than to please Him. We stop "living" to make ourselves righteous and begin to truly live because we **are** truly free. We must return to this grace because all the Christian life flows from it.

> **Ephesians 2:4-7**[62]
> God, who is rich in mercy, **because of His great love with which He loved me**, ⁵ even

---

[62] Personalized by the author

*when I was dead in trespasses, made me **alive**
together with Christ (by grace I have been
saved),* [6] *and raised me up together, and made
me sit together in the heavenly places in Christ
Jesus,* [7] ***that in the ages to come He might
show the exceeding riches of His grace in
His kindness toward me in Christ Jesus.***

It is appropriate for us to know more about God's love. No
matter where you are on your personal journey toward discovering His great love for you, and no matter how you might *feel,*
you can rest in His precious love for you.

Nothing is more important. Without the love of God, there
would be no Savior. Because of His great love with which He
loved us, God will continue demonstrating to us the exceeding
riches of His grace "in the ages to come" in His kindness toward
us in Christ Jesus. This glorious journey of love before us is a
path of joy and peace.

Our entire relationship with God
☙ is based on His love for us. ❧

My friend, God loves you more than you will ever be able
to comprehend. His love for us is our first love. Everything else
flows from His love. He wants us to abide in His love.

So, let us continue our discovery of the height and depth
and width and length of God's unsearchable love. Let us
"behold" it with pure delight. Let us rejoice in it. May we know
and believe it with all of our hearts. Enjoy the journey!

*And we have **known and believed**
the **love** that God has for us.
God is **love**,
and he who abides in **love**
abides in God,
and God in him.*

1 John 4:16

Continuing the Journey

1. Share the ideas that ministered to you most in this book.

Epilogue

Rediscovering His Love for You

*T*here is no end to what we can discover about God's love for us. It was a constant challenge while writing and editing to provide you with what I believe to be the core information to get you on a course of knowing and believing the love God has for you. Even so, there are many things we can still explore. I'd like to give you some suggestions of where to go from here.

Please don't view these as homework or something you *must* do. They are only ideas that I think would be enjoyable. If you prefer to go on your own path or just allow the Holy Spirit to lead you into more of His love, that is perfectly fine.

One suggestion is to read through Genesis - Malachi again with the understanding you gained from this book. Remember to see things in their proper context. Allow yourself to see God as love at all times.

Enjoy the Psalms and Proverbs for what they meant originally, but then adapt them as a New Covenant child of God. Interact with them with singing or even dancing.

Write your own poems or songs about the love of God. If you are an artist of any kind, attempt to depict His love for us.

Create or find home decor that express God's amazing love for us and post it for all to see.

Jesus said, "If you've seen me, you've seen the Father." So, read Matthew, Mark, Luke, and John again. Visualize the life of Christ and open your eyes to how His life, death, and resurrection put God's love on display. Begin to ask, "*Does* this apply to me," instead of, "*How* does this apply to me?"

For those who like journaling, splurge on a new journal and begin to record what you are learning about God's love for you. Or use the journal as a way to converse with God.

Let Him heal you of things in your past that are holding you back from fully knowing and believing the love God has for you. Let him completely set you free. You don't need to spend the rest of your life hurting because of the failures of others. Forgive those who offended you. Look to Jesus and trust Him to comfort you.

Remember His love when sudden and great storms come your way. Don't be afraid. Rest in His love.

Take some time to specifically think about His love for you during the day. Think of clever ways to remember to be thankful and talk with Him. When I look at the time and it is something odd like 2:22, 4:56, 11:11, or 3:21, I often say out loud, "It's 10:10. Time to remember God loves me!" Then I take a minute or two just to enjoy the fact that He really does love me. Yes, me! In between activities, upon waking or when going to bed, talk to Him. Set alarms on your phone if you need to so you will remember to enjoy His presence. Don't feel guilty that you need to remind yourself. This world is designed to distract us, so it's ok to devise some systems to snap back into God's reality. No formulas are required. Just talk to your loving God.

Take a vacation or a few days off at home to focus on the topic of God's great love.

Perhaps you would like to read this book again or study it with a friend. If you are a parent, you could read through these pages with your children or discuss them as you go through life with them. Imagine how different their lives will be because they understand that their God loves them.

Thank-you for taking your precious time to consider the thoughts in this book. Hopefully, you have been blessed. May our beloved God open all of our eyes to the glories of His wonderful love for us throughout our lives.

Sincerely in Jesus,
Cathy Hildebrand

About the Author

Catherine Dalene Hildebrand (1954-) was "raised in church" all her life but tried to abandon her faith in college. Unable to convince herself that God did not exist, she returned to full faith in Christ in 1974. About two years later, she married David. They now have three children and ten grandchildren.

She and David worked in college and youth ministry from 1974-1983. In 1982 they became home missionaries pastoring a church. Unable to find full-time ministry after their mission ended in 1987, they began secular careers.

It was during this same year that Cathy had what she now calls a "grace awakening" which helped her to rediscover her first love in Christ and abandon law-based Christianity. During the years that followed, she worked as an elementary bilingual teacher for four years and then a high school Spanish teacher for eight years while raising three beautiful children.

After this, she and David once again felt God drawing them into ministry. In 2007, she and David founded a church-based Bible institute and were re-ordained by their denomination. It was during this time that she believed God asked her, "Are you willing to preach the gospel to the saved?"

Knowing exactly what He meant she answered, "Yes." In 2009, she and David began a teaching ministry called Studies in Grace and Faith. After three intensive years of studying and teaching the good news to Christians, Catherine was finally ready to publish her first book. Are We Preaching "Another" Gospel?—A 31-Day Journey toward Rediscovering the Gospel of the Grace of God, was written to help believers rediscover the good news of God's amazing grace. Two years later, she composed Overcoming the Overwhelming—A 40-Day Journey toward Rediscovering the Grace of God, to encourage Christians to rediscover faith in God. Her most recent book. Know and Believe, A Lifetime Journey toward Rediscovering God's Love for You was written to encourage believers to feel confident in God's love for them.

Recently, Catherine happily returned to teaching Spanish and English language learners. She currently lives with her dear husband in her beloved Northern California.

Books by C. D. Hildebrand

Are We Preaching "Another" Gospel? (2014)
A 31-Day Journey toward Rediscovering the Gospel of the Grace of God

From the Back of the Book

From the author's perspective the answer to Are We Preaching "Another" Gospel? is a resounding, "Yes." "It isn't that we don't understand the basic tenants of Christianity," she writes, "but that we have added to them."

We used to joyfully proclaim, "Christianity isn't a religion. It's a relationship with Jesus Christ," but if this is so, then why are so many believers today "miserable"? Why do they have a sense that God is far off or lack confidence that He loves them? What happened to the joy they knew "the hour they first believed"? Why does their "relationship" with Jesus actually seem more like a "religion"—a very difficult, demanding, and unsatisfying religion? Why are so many believers, even though they love Jesus with all of their hearts, giving up on "church" or simply attending out of duty or tradition?

The answers to these questions found in the content of this book are challenging—not that they are difficult to under-stand—but that our long-held traditions and false beliefs which keep getting passed on from generation to generation stand in our way of perceiving the truth. Jesus said that knowing the truth would set us free, but if our teaching nullifies that truth, bondage follows. So it is reasonable for us, the church, to consider whether or not what we teach is the "grace of Christ" that sets us free or whether we are preaching "another" gospel which is tying God's people in hundreds of painful and complicated knots.

So, let the journey begin toward rediscovering the "gospel of the grace of God" (Acts 20:24)! Be prepared to be stretched, challenged, and then set free into the glorious good news of your relationship with God.

Overcoming the Overwhelming (2016)
A 40-Day Journey toward Rediscovering Faith in God

From the Back of the Book

There are many challenges we face in life that have simple solutions. Others might take a greater effort, but eventually, we are successful. However, sometimes we experience difficulties that seem beyond our own abilities to overcome. After perhaps years of trying to improve without making any permanent progress, it is easy to feel discouraged and overwhelmed.

It is perplexing to us when we observe that in other areas of our lives we are living victoriously. We might be doing very well in business and relationships and appear to everyone that we "have it all together." Yet, in other facets of our lives, we are still experiencing frustration and defeat.

As the title of the book implies, in order to overcome the overwhelming, we must have faith in God, but how do we find new faith—a faith that will finally help us move "this" mountain?

Jesus said that knowing the truth would set us free. So, first of all, we need to discover what the truth is, especially as it pertains to our overwhelming circumstances. Next, we need to face head-on any thought that is negating the truth or causing us to doubt God's goodness and His loving grace toward us. Then, we simply allow ourselves to believe that God is who He says He is and that He will do what He says He will do, not allowing anything to prevent us from receiving what He has provided.

Set before you in this book is a 40-Day feast of truth that is shared with the objective of setting you free to believe fully in God's kind intentions toward us and receive the victory Jesus won for us. I hope you will be inspired to take this journey toward rediscovering faith in God so that you will finally overcome the overwhelming.

Communications

If you would like to discuss topics about the gospel of the grace of God, having faith in God or rediscovering the love of God for you, feel free to "Like" my Facebook page (C.D. Hildebrand) at https://www.facebook.com/cdhildebrandgrace.

Studies in Grace and Faith

If you are interested in learning more about the topics discussed in these books, or you'd like to engage in a verse by verse study of Scripture, please visit our website at www.graceandfaithministries.org. All video teachings, MP3 recordings, and detailed study notes are available free of charge with new titles in progress.